Collins · *do brilliantly!*

CW01046354

InstantRevisic

GCSE Business Studies

The ideal **solution** to **last-minute** revision

■ **Carolyn Lawder**
■ **Series Editor: Jayne de Courcy**

Contents

Published by HarperCollins*Publishers* Ltd
77-85 Fulham Palace Road
London W6 8JB

www.**Collins**Education.com
On-line support for schools and colleges

First published 2002
This new format edition published 2004
10 9 8 7 6 5 4 3 2
ISBN 0 00 717265 6
Carolyn Lawder asserts the moral right to be identified as the author of this work.

British Library Cataloguing in Publication Data
A catalogue record for this book is available from the British Library.

Edited by Margaret Shepherd
Production by Katie Butler
Design by Gecko Ltd
Illustrations by Gecko Ltd
Cover design by Susi Martin-Taylor
Printed and bound by Printing Express, Hong Kong

Acknowledgements
The Author and Publishers are grateful to the following for permission to reproduce
copyright material:
Burger King 5
McDonald's 5
The Body Shop 5

Photographs
Allsport 62
Hulton Archive 70
Maximilian Stock Ltd/Science Photo Library 72

Every effort has been made to contact the holders of copyright material, but if any
have been inadvertently overlooked, the Publishers will be pleased to make the
necessary arrangements at the first opportunity.

Get the most out of your Instant Revision pocket book

1 **Maximise your revision time.** You can carry this book around with you anywhere. This means you can spend any spare moments dipping into it.

2 **Learn and remember what you need to know.** This book contains all the really important facts you need to know for your exam. All the information is set out clearly and concisely, making it easy for you to revise.

3 **Find out what you don't know.** The *Check yourself* questions and *Score chart* help you to see quickly and easily the topics you're good at and those you're not so good at.

What's in this book

1 The facts – just what you need to know

- The chapters cover all the core Business Studies topics set by the Exam Boards.
- The information is presented in short blocks so that it is easy to read and remember.

2 *Check yourself* questions – find out how much you know and boost your grade

- Each chapter ends with a *Check yourself* page.
- The questions are quick to answer. They aren't actual exam questions but they will show you what you do and don't know.

- The answers are given at the end of the book. Don't cheat! Try to work out all the answers before turning to the back.

- There are points for each question. The total number of points for each *Check yourself* is always 20. When you check your answers, fill in the score box alongside each answer with the number of points you feel you scored.

3 The *Score chart* – an instant picture of your strengths and weaknesses

- *Score chart (1)* lists all the *Check yourself* pages.

- As you complete each *Check yourself*, record your points on the *Score chart*. This will show you instantly which areas you need to spend more time on.

- *Score chart (2)* is a graph which lets you plot your points against GCSE grades. This will give you a rough idea of how you are doing in each area. Of course, this is only a rough idea because the questions aren't real exam questions!

Use this Instant Revision pocket book on your own – or revise with a friend or relative. See who can get the highest score!

Sole trader

- A sole trader is also known as a **sole proprietor**.

- A sole trader is the single owner of a business and makes all the decisions. Sole traders are responsible if anything goes wrong.

- A sole trader has **unlimited liability**. This means that if the business fails the owner is responsible for all the debts of the business and may lose their possessions.

- Not a great deal of capital is needed to start up the business but it can make it harder for the business to grow.

- Because sole trader businesses are often small, they may suffer from some disadvantages.
  - They may not gain **economies of scale** because they cannot buy in bulk, so pay more for their goods.
  - They may not benefit from **specialisation** and **division of labour**. In a small business with few employees, people will have to do more than one job and not just the one they are best at.

- The aims of the sole trader will not just be to make a profit. Sole traders may be in business so that they can make all the decisions and have the lifestyle that they want. They may just aim to survive.

- The sole trader *is* the business, so the business will have **lack of continuity**. If the owner of the business dies, then that is the end of that business.

Partnership

- A partnership is an agreement between two or more people to own and take responsibility for a business.

- What is shared?
  - The money needed to start up the business
  - Ownership
  - Liability for any debts
  - Profit
  - Decisions
  - The jobs that need doing
  - Knowledge and skills.

- Usually a **deed of partnership** is drawn up. This is a legal document that includes:
  - how much money each partner will put in to start the business
  - how profits and losses are to be shared
  - what each partner will have responsibility for
  - how the partnership will be ended.

  Having a deed of partnership can prevent problems and disagreements in the future.

- Partnerships have **unlimited liability** which means a partner could be responsible for some debts even if they were caused by another partner.

- Partnerships have a **lack of continuity**. If one of the partners dies, then the partnership is ended.

- Partnerships usually have more capital then sole traders so an aim may be to **expand**, as well as to survive and make a **profit**.

- Disagreements between the partners may make decision-making difficult.

- Having to share profit means that the person who does the most work may not be the one who gets the greatest reward.

Limited companies

- There are two types of limited companies:
  - **Private limited companies** (Ltd)
  - **Public limited companies** (Plc).

- The most important difference between private and public limited companies is that shares in private limited companies **cannot be sold to the general public**.

- Limited companies get their capital by issuing shares. For each share bought there is an **equal** amount of ownership, an **equal** amount of say in the running of the business and an **equal** share in any profits.

- Limited companies have **limited liability**. This means that if the business has debts, the owners are only responsible for the amount of capital that they put into the business (the amount of money that they paid for the shares that they bought).

- The business has **legal entity** which means that it exists in its own right. There is a lot of legal documentation required by businesses before they can be set up. This includes registering the business with the Registrar of Companies and drawing up a Memorandum of Association. A Memorandum of Association must include the type of limited company, name, address, purpose of the company and amount of capital to be raised.

- A public limited company is able to sell shares on the stock exchange. This means it has access to much more **capital**.

- The person originally setting up the limited company can lose control of the business because there is a **divorce of ownership and control**. The owners appoint directors who appoint managers all of whom may have different aims for the business.

Ownership and control

1 What does unlimited liability mean? (3)

2 What is another name for a sole trader? (1)

3 Which types of business have a lack of continuity? (2)

4 What is meant by economies of scale? (2)

5 Which of the three types of business:
   ■ sole trader
   ■ partnership
   ■ limited company

   is most likely to suffer from lack of specialisation and division of labour? (1)

6 Explain what is usually included in a deed of partnership. (4)

7 What are the two types of limited company? (2)

8 In a limited company who gets a share of the profit? (1)

9 In a sole trader business who makes all the decisions? (1)

10 In which type of business do the owners have limited liability? (1)

11 What is meant by legal entity? (1)

12 Which type of business has legal entity? (1)

The answers are on page 102.

Franchises

- A **franchise** exists when a company sells to another business the right to use their name and sell their goods and services.

- A **franchisee** is the person who buys the right to use the name and pays a fee to the **franchiser**.

- The franchisee gains because he has to spend less money than if he had developed his own products and brand name. There is also lower risk for the franchisee because the name and products are established.

- The franchiser gains because he can expand with lower costs and still retain control.

- The franchisee may not like the fact that he has less control. He will have to keep to a set of rules. The franchiser makes all the product designs and marketing decisions.

- The franchisee pays a royalty on the year's **turnover** (the total sales revenue) and will have to pay this whether there is any profit or not. If there is a profit he will get to keep it.

- Many well-known **brands** are franchises:

Co-operatives

- A **co-operative** business is one in which a group of people come together to trade, for the benefit of all those in the group.

- A co-operative can be made up of workers, consumers or producers.

- Examples of co-operatives are Café Direct and Sunkist.

- In worker co-operatives there are fewer chances of industrial relations problems as there are no conflicts of objectives. The workers are usually well motivated because they are working for themselves.

- However, it is hard for co-operatives to expand because the more members there are, the harder it is to make decisions.

- Members of co-operatives become involved in making decisions about which they may have no knowledge or experience.

Public sector organisations

- The public sector is any organisation that is owned by the government and run on behalf of the people.

- The Army, the BBC and the Post Office are examples of public sector organisations.

- Some services are public sector because they are considered to be vital, for example, the National Health Service.

- **Privatisation** means putting public sector organisations into private hands.

Privatisation	
For	**Against**
Encourages people to own shares.	Monopolies are created which may charge too much.
Decisions are made faster.	Decisions may not be in the best interests of the public because profit may be the motive.
Costs the government less.	Private companies may not invest enough money in something that is vital for the public.
Increases competition.	Competition can waste money because more than one business is providing the service.
Increases efficiency.	Job losses.

● **Nationalisation** means taking a private business into public ownership, that is, into a public sector organisation. Do *not* confuse public sector organisations with public limited companies.

● Nationalisation has not been popular with governments as it is seen as telling the public what they need rather than giving them the choice of a range of services.

● Nationalisation means that the money needed to run the organisations usually comes from taxes. This can be unpopular as not everyone benefits equally from the service and some people may contribute who do not directly use the service at all.

Forms of business

1 What is a franchise? (1)

2 Which of these are advantages of being a franchise? (2)

    A There is less risk because products are well known.

    B The franchiser has unlimited liability.

    C The franchiser uses national advertising.

    D The franchisee can make all the decisions.

3 Over what things will a franchisee have no control? (2)

4 What is meant by turnover? (1)

5 Give two examples of a franchise. (2)

6 Name three types of co-operative. (3)

7 Why are some services in the public sector? (1)

8 Which of the following are public sector organisations? (2)

    A Tesco

    B BBC

    C The Body Shop

    D The Army

9 What does nationalisation mean? (1)

10 What are the reasons for privatisation? (5)

The answers are on page 103.

● **Stakeholders** are people or organisations that have a financial interest in a business.

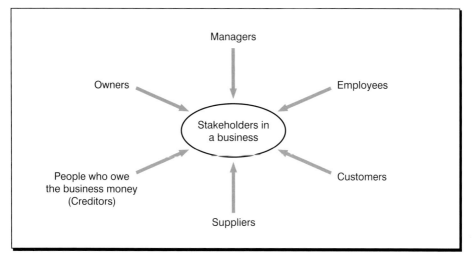

Owners' objectives

● The usual objectives for the owners of businesses are:
  ■ survival
  ■ profit
  ■ growth.

● Businesses in their early years often state that they aim to survive, as the first few years in business are the hardest. At this stage, businesses are attempting to **penetrate the market** and obtain a **share of the market** for their goods and services. That means they wish to try and attract some sales from the existing businesses.

● To begin with, a business may have the objective to **break even**. This means that sales revenue will equal the total costs. No profit will be made but there will be no loss either.

● Objectives usually change after the early years. After the first year, objectives are usually to make or increase the profit.

- After the early years, a business may wish to expand. This expansion can be by increasing either the range of products or the number of locations. This will hopefully lead to **maximising sales** and **maximising profit**. Maximising means making the most of something.

- Sole traders may have different objectives and may be more interested in **satisficing**. **Satisficing** means reaching a certain level or target but not necessarily making the most of anything. The objectives may be to do with lifestyle rather than making as much profit as possible.

Other stakeholders' objectives

- Managers may have the same objectives as the owners, especially if they are rewarded for achieving profit. If they are not directly rewarded then they may want to increase their own status.

- Suppliers are likely to want to have repeat orders so they want the business to be reliable so it can pay their bills when they are due.

- Employees will want reasonable pay and good, safe working conditions. They will want the business to survive because they want to keep their jobs.

- Creditors will want to be paid the money that is owed to them.

- Customers will want a good product and value for money. They will also want the business to survive – they want the business to be reliable so that they can have after-sales service should anything go wrong.

Conflicts in objectives	
Employees want more pay.	Owners want to reduce costs.
Customers want low prices.	Owners want more profits.
Suppliers want to be paid on time.	Owners want to delay payment.
Customers want a high quality product.	Owners want to reduce costs.

Growth

- A business can be measured in size in a variety of ways:
  - sales turnover
  - % market share
  - number of employees
  - value of the business
  - the number of locations it covers.

- If a business is able to grow, it may benefit from **economies of scale**. For example, savings may be made in buying raw materials if they arc bought in large quantities.

- A business may have market domination as its aim. That means it aims to have the greatest market share so that it can set prices.

- Growth can be achieved through internal or external methods.
  - **Internal growth** means becoming larger from within the business.
  - **External growth** is expanding by taking over other businesses.

- External growth can be achieved through **mergers**. This is where two companies of similar size join together. Another means is by **take-overs** where one business is taken over by another.

- If a firm controls a large part of a market, is able to control the price structure and prevent competitors surviving, it is said to have a **monopoly**. Any take-overs or mergers planned by a monopoly are usually subject to government control.

Check yourself

Objectives and growth

1 Match each term with its meaning. (3)

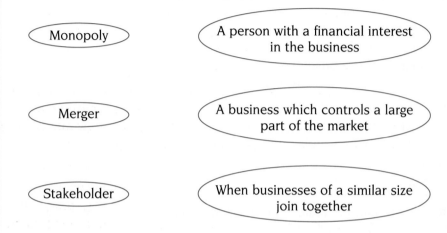

Monopoly — A person with a financial interest in the business

Merger — A business which controls a large part of the market

Stakeholder — When businesses of a similar size join together

2 Who are the usual stakeholders in a business? (6)

3 What is the difference between satisficing and maximising? (2)

4 What objectives do owners usually have for their businesses? (3)

5 Explain two objectives for employees in a business. (2)

6 Explain how a customer's objectives may conflict with those of the owner. (2)

7 What are the two main types of growth? (2)

The answers are on page 104.

- Recruitment and selection of staff is about finding and choosing the best possible employees to work for an organisation.

- The process begins with advertising in the best place. This will be different for each type of job. Possible places to advertise include: internal notice board, external notice board, job centre, local radio, local newspaper and national newspapers.

- Where a business advertises will depend on how much it can afford and from how far away people will consider applying for the job. For example, for a local part-time unskilled job, employers would be wasting resources by advertising in the national press. They will also need to think about whether enough of the right people will see the advertisement.

- The next stage is to think about the content of the advertisement. There is certain information that must be given. The advertisement below gives the basic information.

BEST BURGERS
Welchurch

Required as soon as possible energetic full-time staff to deal with the growing demand for burgers in Welchurch. You must be fit, enthusiastic and willing to work varied shifts.

Pay is above local rates and a free uniform is provided.

If you are interested, please contact William Lawder on **01944 666000** for an application form.

- Most businesses will ask candidates to write a letter of application and/or fill in an application form giving details of their age, qualifications and experience. They will also ask for references. Some businesses will ask for a **CV**. A CV is a curriculum vitae which gives an account of your life to date.

- The personnel manager will study the application forms and other documents in order to select the candidates who meet the criteria for the job.

- From the application form or CV they will produce a **shortlist** of candidates to interview. The shortlist will usually contain less than ten candidates. At the interview the candidates will be asked a number of questions about their skills, interests and other experience they have. They may possibly be given some tests such as mental arithmetic, IT or an aptitude test to see if they would be able to do the job.

- References will then be taken up so that past employers can give an accurate picture of how the candidates performed in the workplace. School leavers will need a reference from the head teacher of the school.

- Once appointed, employees are given a contract of employment. This will include:
  - job title and starting date
  - payment method
  - hours of work and holiday/sickness benefits
  - period of notice required on leaving the job
  - pension arrangements.

Recruitment and selection

1 In what three ways might people be asked to apply for a job? (3)

2 What is a CV? (1)

3 What is a shortlist? (2)

4 Describe the other methods an organisation might use to select from the applicants. (4)

5 What factors do you need to take into account when choosing where to advertise a vacancy? (3)

6 Which four important pieces of information are missing in this job advertisement? (4)

7 List three items that should be included on a contract of employment. (3)

The answers are on page 105.

Why do businesses train their employees?

- Training can introduce new employees to the business. This is called **induction training**.

- Dangers in the workplace need to be explained to all workers so that the business ensures the **health and safety** of its employees. Health and Safety law demands that employees and employers share the responsibility for keeping a safe workplace. Training shows that the employers take this responsibility seriously.

- Training can **motivate** employees and can be the means for them getting promotion to a better job. This is usually known as **staff development**. Motivating means encouraging the employees to do the job as well as they can.

- Businesses try to improve their **efficiency**. This means that they try to increase their output from the resources that they have. By training their employees, they hope to increase the amount produced by each worker.

- New technology is often introduced to try and increase the efficiency. When it is introduced, it means that employees need training on how to use it. Some employees will need to be retrained so that they can remain in employment as new technology takes over from existing machinery. This also contributes to increased efficiency.

Induction training

- Induction training is needed to introduce the new employee to:
  - the business
  - the workplace
  - the job.

Content	Reason
Information about the company	New employees need to know the aims and objectives and the types of products it makes. This makes the employee feel part of the company.
Health and Safety	It is important that from the start the employee is able to be a safe member of the workforce. The law states that the employee has a responsibility for Health and Safety as well as the employer.
Tour of the company	The new employee needs to know the location of certain areas within the business, such as canteen facilities, fire exits and lockers where personal possessions can be stored.
Introduction to key personnel such as co-workers and supervisors	The employee needs to know who to ask when help is needed and who they are directly responsible to.
Identification of any training needs	The new employee may be assessed to see if he needs any further training before he can begin work.

Methods of training

● Training can be either **on the job** or **off the job**.

● On-the-job training takes place within the business at the site of the employee's new job. This can be the actual production line where the employee is working or the office where he works.

● Off-the-job training takes place away from the workplace, possibly still at the business premises but in a separate training area. Alternatively it may take place away from the site altogether.

On-the-job training

- This is cheaper – no special premises required to be hired or built.

- It is more relevant – the employee can see how it directly relates to his job.

- It uses existing skilled employees – these people have experience of doing things the way the business wants them done.

- It can be a motivator for those doing the training.

Off-the-job training

- This can use specialist instructors – people who are skilled at showing others how to do the job, not just good at the job themselves.

- Training can lead to a recognised qualification such as NVQ 2 – this can benefit the employee and can encourage him to stay in the company.

- The use of a training environment can motivate people if it is a pleasant training or conference centre. The training can take place in a College of Further or Higher Education.

- Any mistakes that the trainee makes are unlikely to affect the reputation of the business. Goods made at a training centre are not part of the production line and therefore not sold to the public.

- The training can be flexible in length. For example, it can be one day a week or a whole block of time without affecting the productivity of the production line.

Training

1 Why is Health and Safety training needed? (2)

2 What is induction training? (1)

3 Which is the best definition of efficiency? (1)

   A Increases input with the resources they have.

   B Increases output with the resources they have.

   C Uses new resources to increase output.

4 Why is information about the company needed on an induction course? (3)

5 Who are 'key personnel'? (2)

6 Name three areas you would show a new worker on a tour of the workplace. (3)

7 Which type of training takes place away from the actual production line? (1)

8 What are the advantages of using on-the-job training? (4)

9 How can training motivate employees (3)

The answers are on page 106.

- Motivation means encouraging the workers to do the job as well as they can.

- It is vital for a company to motivate its workers because:
  - The workers will work harder and be more efficient.
  - They will be less likely to take time off work unnecessarily. If workers stay away without good cause it is known as **absenteeism**.
  - They will be less likely to be late.
  - They will be more likely to stay with the company for longer.

  All of these reasons save the company money because more will be produced. Also it will save money on recruiting new workers and training them.

- There are several theories as to why workers are prepared to work harder. The most common theories you will find are those of Maslow, McGregor and Herzberg.

Maslow's theory

- Maslow believed that there was a hierarchy of needs. Each level had to be met before the next one could be achieved.

- In his view the most basic need was **survival**. All employees require a basic level of pay in order to survive. For many workers, pay remains the most important reason for work. Pay means that workers can afford to have food and shelter.

- Once workers have enough money to survive, they need to feel **secure** – to know that if they are sick they will still be safe.

● The third level of the hierarchy is **social** needs. People tend to want to feel that they belong to a group. Some businesses are keen that workers feel that they belong to a family and are important to the business. This is shown in larger organisations by the formation of a Social or Sports club. Small businesses may have nights out or a special Christmas dinner.

● The next level is **status** – increasing the personal reputation of the worker. People need to feel that they are respected members of the workforce. Giving workers a say in decision-making often increases their status. Other means include allowing training to a higher level, perhaps management training. For managers, perks such as a good quality company car can show status.

● **Self-actualisation**, the highest level, means achieving the most that is possible for the individual. People will set themselves aims and try and reach them. Employers can help their workers achieve this by providing targets and opportunities for promotion. Ordinary production workers can be given the chance to be promoted to supervisor.

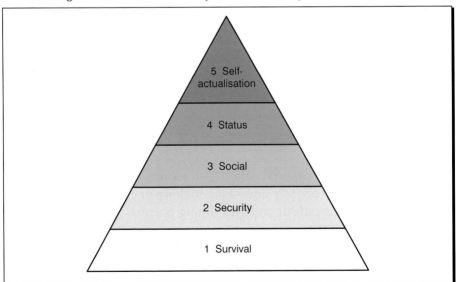

Maslow's hierarchy of needs

Herzberg

- Herzberg identified things that motivated people as: doing a job well, being shown trust, being given responsibility, appreciation and promotion.

- He identified **hygiene factors** – things that made employees **demotivated** if they were not present at work, but which did not, themselves, increase motivation. These included pay and good working conditions. Demotivated means made to work less hard. Herzberg believed that if you increased pay you did not necessarily increase motivation but poor pay would make workers demotivated.

McGregor

- McGregor studied the way that employers and employees thought of work. Some people believed in theory X and some in theory Y. He thought that managers who believed in theory Y would have better-motivated workers.

- If you believed in theory X you would think that workers:
  - dislike work so do as little as possible
  - only work for the pay
  - need to be told exactly what to do and not given any decisions to make
  - will resist any changes the employer wishes to make
  - cannot be trusted or relied upon.

- If you believed in theory Y you would think that workers:
  - like their work
  - are motivated by rewards other than money
  - will work independently and enjoy making decisions
  - will enjoy being part of changes taking place
  - are trustworthy and reliable.

Motivation

1 What are the four main reasons for companies wanting to motivate their workers? (4)

2 How does motivating the workers save the company money? (2)

3 Put these Maslow's needs in their correct order. (5)

Status   Security   Survival   Self-actualisation   Social

4 How might a company that believes in Maslow's hierarchy of needs try to meet an employee's needs for status? (2)

5 What are hygiene factors? (2)

6 If you followed Herzberg's theory, suggest one thing you could do to try and improve motivation? (1)

7 Complete this sentence.

McGregor believed that theory ___ would mean workers were better motivated. (1)

8 Which is true about McGregor's theory? (1)

A He believed that theory X workers enjoyed doing as little as possible.

B He believed a follower of theory X would think that workers enjoyed doing as little as possible.

C He thought the way to motivate workers was to give them as little work as was possible.

9 What else could be included in this job advertisement to show that the company believed in theory Y? (2)

WANTED TRAINEE MANAGERS
Can you work on your own? Are you keen and enthusiastic?
We offer the chance to work in a rapidly expanding young company.
Phone 01122 666996 for further details.

The answers are on page 107.

- Employees can be rewarded by **pay**, **fringe benefits** or **incentives**. Fringe benefits are commonly known as 'perks' and are extras other than money. Incentives include giving payment linked to output or performance.

- Pay may not be the best method of motivation but a good rate of pay may prevent workers from being demotivated. It can be one of the factors involved in people changing their jobs if the other aspects of the job are similar.

- The method of paying workers can be chosen to make people work harder.

Methods of payment

- The main methods of payment are: time rate, piece rate, bonus payments.

Time rate

- Workers are paid for the number of hours taken to do the job. The pay is normally given as an hourly rate for production workers, for example £4.50 per hour. For certain staff the pay will be given as an annual salary, for example £13 000 per year.

- **Advantages**
  - It is simple to operate and can be used easily with time clocks where workers 'clock in' and 'clock out' at either end of the day.
  - It is easy to compare the rates of pay given by different employers.
  - If the job cannot be completed in the normal working hours, the rate of pay can be increased. This is known as **overtime pay**. Workers are often prepared to stay for extra time or work on a day they do not usually work if they are paid time-and-a-half or double pay for it. Some workers rely on overtime to increase their pay.

- **Disadvantages**
  - It can encourage workers to work slowly during normal time so that they can be given overtime. This can be very expensive for employers.
  - There is no reference to quality. As long as the workers are there, they will get paid, even if the quality of what they do is not very good.

Piece rate

- This means that workers are paid according to how many items they produce. Usually these items have to be of a certain quality standard otherwise they do not count in the total.

- **Advantages**
  - It encourages people to work at a fast speed and so more goods are produced.

- **Disadvantages**
  - It can be difficult to administer fairly if the system of production is complicated. If teams are involved then all the team may suffer if someone does not produce enough.
  - It encourages speed rather than careful work. More rejects will be produced using this system.

Bonus payments

- These can be paid for a variety of reasons including: attendance, punctuality, completing work by a certain time or quality.

- **Advantages**
  - Can be a good motivator for the stated reasons providing the bonus is a worthwhile amount.
  - Can be used to help sort out problems like persistent lateness by the workforce.

- **Disadvantages**
  - Workers can come to rely on these bonuses and expect to get them for just doing the job.

Perks

- Many sales or management jobs are advertised with a salary and 'benefits' or 'perks'. Many perks are taxed by the government but are still valued by the employees.

• SALES MANAGER •
Lancashire area
Expanding food company
Attractive salary + benefits
Company car

- Perks can include: company cars, free or cheap travel, health insurance, cheap mortgages, subsidised canteen, computer, discounts on products and telephone allowances.

- It is important that the perks match the status of the job. It is not likely that a production worker would be given a company car.

Incentives

- Workers at all levels can be paid incentives for meeting targets. This is known as **performance-related pay**. Should a worker achieve or exceed his target he will be paid an additional sum.

- Another common incentive is to pay sales staff a **commission** on their sales, that is, to pay a % of the value of the sales.

- Some workers are also paid profit-related pay, thereby encouraging the worker to contribute to the overall profit of the business.

Rewarding employees

1 What are the three main ways of rewarding employees? (3)

2 Match the correct method of payment with its description. (3)

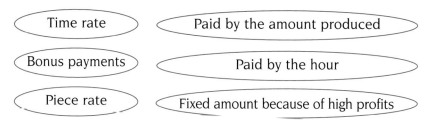

Time rate

Paid by the amount produced

Bonus payments

Paid by the hour

Piece rate

Fixed amount because of high profits

3 What is the name for the payment made if hours have to be worked above the normal ones? (1)

4 If a worker is paid overtime at time-and-a-half calculate his overtime rate per hour if his normal hourly pay is £5. (1)

5 Which methods of payment are least likely to improve quality on a production line? (2)

6 What methods of payments are most likely to be given to managers? (2)

7 What are the most likely perks that a skilled production worker might be given? (2)

8 Is commission a perk or an incentive? (1) Why? (1)

9 What is performance-related pay? (2)

10 What would you expect the salary package to include for this job? (2)

Personnel Director
required for

Successful Engineering Company

North East England

Good salary package

The answers are on page 108.

- A business can need money for various reasons throughout its life. There are major stages when a business may need money:

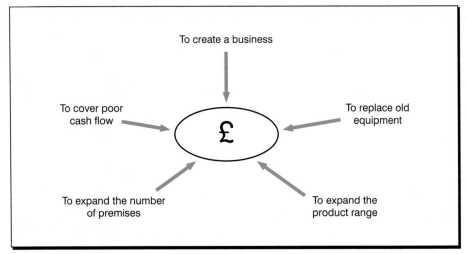

- There can be only two types of finance available to a business:
  - **internal**, from within the business
  - **external**, from sources outside the business.

Owner's funds

- Owner's funds are a form of internal finance. A new business may use money from its owner – this may include redundancy pay or personal savings. An existing business may use profit it obtained in previous years. When this has been kept in the business it is known as **retained profit**.

- If a limited company is set up then the owners become shareholders with a right to have a say in the running of the company and a share of the profits in return for their investment of capital in the business.

- The major advantage of owner's funds is that the business does not have to pay any interest on the money.

- A **sole trader** can increase his capital by putting in more of his own money or looking for a partner to join the business. However, this means he will then have to share decisions and profits.

- A **partnership** can add additional partners to the business to obtain more funds.

- A **private or public limited company** can sell additional shares. If this is to new shareholders it will mean sharing the profit between more people.

Grants

- Grants can be obtained from a wide range of sources. However, only some geographical areas and types of business qualify for particular grants. The grants also vary greatly in value. Some are linked directly to an aspect of business, for example, for marketing or for diversification.

- Providers of grants include charities like the Prince's Trust, the local council, the government and the EC.

Borrowed funds

- Money can be borrowed for a variety of lengths of time. These are related to the purpose the money is needed for. These lengths of time are a guide as some lenders use slightly different times:

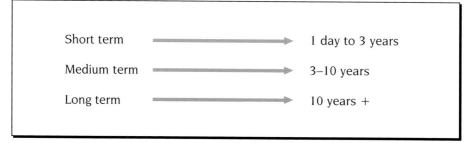

Short term	→	1 day to 3 years
Medium term	→	3–10 years
Long term	→	10 years +

Short term

- Short-term needs are usually to cover cash flow problems during which a business has little cash coming in for a short while. An example might be an ice cream producer who needs to still pay his rent in winter despite few sales.

- Sources include:

Overdraft	An agreement with the bank to spend up to a certain limit. Interest is only charged on the amount borrowed.
Bank loan	A set amount is borrowed for a certain amount of time. Interest is charged on the full amount borrowed until the end of the loan.
Trade credit	Goods are bought and paid for after a delay of usually 30 days but it can be longer. No interest is usually charged.

Medium term

- Medium-term loans are used to cover particular purchases by businesses such as replacing worn out machinery, developing a new product or investing in new technology.

- Sources include:

Bank loan	A set amount is borrowed for a certain amount of time. Interest is charged on the full amount borrowed until the end of the loan.
Hire purchase or leasing	Equipment is bought in the case of hire purchase or leased (not owned) over a period of years and paid for in instalments. Interest is added to the amount paid.

Long term

- This type of finance would be used to pay for setting up a new business or a large-scale expansion. It can be used to pay for buildings or assets that will last for the length of the loan.

- Sources include:

Long-term loans	As for medium-term loan but the lender will make sure that he has sufficient security against the loan.
Mortgage	Loan used for land and buildings. Usually for very large sums of money. Can be a fixed or variable interest rate.
Sale and leaseback	Land or buildings may be sold to a company and then leased back. Interest is charged and the business no longer owns the asset.
Debentures	Large public companies can borrow through the City of London. Interest is charged but may be less than other lenders.

Case study
A typical small business

Jane's Café

Jane Whitchurch used her redundancy money and her savings to set up her café in 1993. She was able to obtain a mortgage lasting 25 years for the building. She was able to lease the majority of her kitchen equipment from a specialist shop. The food she needed was bought from a wholesaler, who gave her 30 days trade credit.

After five years steady trade she decided to use some of the profit she had retained over the years to expand her business. She decided to obtain a medium-term bank loan and buy another café in a nearby town. She used an overdraft to help her cash flow problems, whilst she spent a large sum of money advertising her new premises.

Sources of finance

1 Name the main reasons why a business may need to find finance. (5)

2 Complete this sentence.

Finance can be internal or _____ . (1)

3 Which of the following is retained profit? (1)

   A Money left in the bank

   B Profit from previous years kept in the business

   C Profit given to the shareholders

4 How can a partnership get additional owner's funds? (2)

5 What is the main advantage of using owner's funds? (1)

6 Which of the following are short-term sources of finance? (2)

   A Trade credit

   B Debentures

   C Overdraft

   D Leasing of premises

   E Mortgage of land

   F Hire purchase of machinery

7 Name three sources of grants to businesses. (3)

8 What are the main disadvantages for a limited company raising funds by selling additional shares? (2)

9 Suggest three ways a business could finance an expansion. (3)

The answers are on page 109.

What is a business plan?

- A business plan is a document produced before a business is created, giving details of all aspects of the proposed business. The owners usually write the plan, often with help given by advisors from the banks or business advisors.

What does a business plan contain?

- A business plan would include the following:

Content	Reasons
Names, addresses and contact numbers of owners	So that anyone looking at the plan can contact them
Business structure: sole trader, partnership, etc	So that others, such as a bank, can see who is the owner and thus responsible for the business
Aims and objectives	So that the owners and managers can see what the targets are and any key dates for the business
Market research	So that possible investors can see if there is proven demand for the goods and the business is likely to succeed
Marketing information	Details of the proposed marketing mix, to assess its likely chances of success and if it is affordable
Details of the proposed products or services and an analysis of the competition	To see if enough thought has gone into making the product/service unique
Staffing	To see if the proposed staffing is able to cover all major jobs within the business and that not too much is being spent on staff
Financial information, accurate details of assets owned by the business and liabilities. Forecasts of cash flow and break even	To help determine the likely chance of running into difficulties. A bank would want to see that the information and predictions were realistic.

How owners can use a business plan

- The owners will use the business plan as a checklist when setting up their business. They will probably obtain a pro-forma from a bank or advisor and can use this to make sure that they do not leave anything out when planning their business.

- Once the business is up and running the owners can refer to their targets and strive to meet them. They can compare their performance with what was predicted and look for the reasons why they met or otherwise the targets.

- The existing owners could also show the business plan to prospective investors. The quality of the business plan could persuade them to invest in the business and join it by becoming shareholders or partners.

- The plan could be shown to the bank or other lenders to persuade them to grant a loan.

How a bank manager can use a business plan

- The bank manager needs to make sure that the business idea will work and that any money he lends will be safe. He therefore needs to make sure that the business will not fail.

- He will assess if the product or service has been thought through and is very likely to be demanded by the public.

- He will also need to check that the product and the marketing plans compare well with the competition.

- By looking at the staffing and details of the owners, he will try and assess if the business has enough people with the right skills.

Business plans

1 What is a business plan? (2)

2 How is a business plan used after the business has begun trading? (2)

3 Which of the following items would not appear on a business plan? (2)

    A Names, addresses and contact numbers of owners

    B Business structure: sole trader, partnership, etc.

    C Value of goods sold last month

    D Market research

    E Copies of recent advertisements

4 What information is needed concerning the assets owned by the business? (2)

5 Name two financial forecasts included in the business plan. (2)

6 Why would a bank manager want to see if enough market research had been done? (2)

7 What must the financial data be on a business plan? (2)

8 What should the owners investigate regarding the competition? (2)

9 Give four reasons why future owners and managers would want to see a business plan. (4)

The answers are on page 110.

Types of costs

- When a business makes a product or gives a service there is a wide range of inputs that go into it. The business has to pay for these and they are known as **costs**.

- **Fixed costs (FC)** are those costs that do not vary directly with output. In making the cup of tea the cost of the teapot will stay the same whether we make one cup of tea or three cups. Even if we make no tea today we will still have paid for the teapot.

- Typical fixed costs include:
  - rent or costs of premises
  - rates
  - interests on loans
  - equipment.

- **Variable costs (VC)** are those costs that vary directly with output. In making the cup of tea, the cost of the tea will vary according to how many cups we make. One cup of tea uses one tea bag; three cups use three tea bags. If we make no tea we will not use any tea bags at all.

- Typical variable costs include:
  - ingredients or parts
  - packaging
  - wages of production workers.

- Some costs can be fixed or variable depending on the type of business. The electricity used for boiling the kettle will vary according to how much water we put in the kettle. However we will have to put on the lights in the café and heat it even if we don't have any customers. Therefore electricity can be a fixed cost and a variable one.

- Wages can also be fixed or variable costs. Normally in a production business we say that direct labour is a variable cost and that the management and office staff are fixed costs.

- **Start-up costs** are costs that occur when a new business is begun.

- Typical start-up costs include:
  - fitting premises
  - equipment costs
  - decoration of premises.

- **Running costs** are costs that occur once a business has begun to sell its goods or services.

- Typical running costs include:
  - raw materials or ingredients
  - electricity
  - wages
  - postage and packing.

- Some costs can be both start-up and running costs. These include advertising – when done for the launch of a business it is a start-up cost but after that it becomes a running cost.

- Costs of stock can also be both a start-up and running costs, as again stock is needed for the launch and to carry on trading.

- **Total costs (TC)** are the total of *fixed costs* and *variable costs*.
- **Revenue** is the money coming into the business from the sale of the goods or services. It is the business's income before any costs are considered.
- **Total revenue (TR)** is the *price of the product × quantity sold*.
- **Break even** is the level of sales needed for *total costs* to equal *total revenue*.
- Break even can be worked out by either using a formula or by drawing a graph. The formula for break even is:

$$\frac{fixed\ costs}{price\ per\ unit - variable\ cost\ per\ unit}$$

- Another name for (*price per unit – variable cost per unit*) is **contribution**.

Case study

Oldie Pine Ltd makes and sells reproduction pine farmhouse tables. The cost of the reclaimed pine is £35 per table. Wages are £15 per table. Fixed costs were £16 250 per year. The tables are sold at £115 each. Calculate the quantity of tables that must be sold to break even.

Fixed costs £16 250
Variable costs are £35 + £15 = £50
Price per unit is £115

$$\frac{Fixed\ costs}{Price\ per\ unit - Variable\ cost\ per\ unit} = \frac{£16\,250}{£115 - £50}$$
$$= 250\ tables\ per\ year$$

● Break even can be plotted on a graph by first completing a table.

Break-even table

Sales	FC	VC	TC	TR
0	16 250	0	16 250	0
50	16 250	2500	18 750	5750
100	16 250	5000	21 250	11 500
150	16 250	7500	23 750	17 250
200	16 250	10 000	26 250	23 000
250	16 250	12 500	28 750	28 750

● This graph would then be drawn:

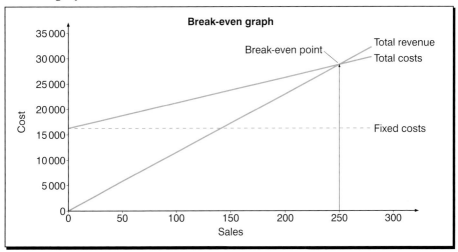

Why calculate break even?

● The break-even point is the point where neither a loss or a profit is made. Therefore a business can see at what point a profit will be made and this can become a target.

● The business can see if the break-even point is possible to attain. It can use the calculation to spot likely problems such as too high a figure for fixed costs.

● The business can study the effect of changing costs and revenues.

Break even

1 Match the cost with its definition. (5)

Running cost — Cost that varies with the amount produced

Total costs — Costs that occur when the business is trading

Variable cost — Sum of fixed and variable costs

Setting-up cost — Costs that remain the same however many items are produced

Fixed cost — Costs involved in setting up a business

2 Name two costs that can be both a fixed and a variable cost. (2)

3 Why is it helpful for a business to know its break-even point? (3)

4 Copy and complete the table. (5)

Break-even table for pine chairs				
Sales	FC	VC	TC	TR
0	2500	0	2500	0
25		250		1500
50	2500	500	3000	
75	2500			4500

5 Calculate the break-even point for bedside tables from this data. (5)

Fixed costs = £900

Cost of wages per table = £6

Cost of wood per table = £4

Selling price per table = £25

The answers are on page 111.

- Cash flow is:
  - **inflows**, money coming into a business
  - **outflows**, money going out of a business.

- A **cash flow forecast** is a prediction of the future inflows and outflows of money over a period of time, usually a year.

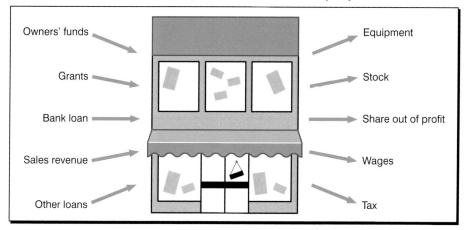

Owners' funds
Grants
Bank loan
Sales revenue
Other loans

Equipment
Stock
Share out of profit
Wages
Tax

- On any particular day it is not very likely that the cash inflows will exactly equal the cash outflows. If there are more inflows then the business is said to have a cash **surplus**. More outflows will give a cash **deficit**.

- Many businesses that fail do not do so because their products are poor or they are unprofitable. They do so because they do not have enough money to pay their bills at that particular time.

- A cash flow forecast helps a business predict when it is likely to have cash deficits. It is then able to plan for them by perhaps taking out a loan or arranging an overdraft to cover the period of shortage. A bank manager would expect to see a cash flow forecast before agreeing to any loans.

- It is also helpful for the business to compare the actual cash flow with what was predicted. The business can then see when it can afford to pay people it owes money to and when it can consider buying more stock or equipment.

- A cash flow forecast can be shown as a table.

	Jan	Feb	Mar	Apr	May
Bank balance b/f	1000	5000	3000	−1000	1000
Cash receipts	12 000	10 000	8000	8000	10 000
Total cash in	13 000	15 000	11 000	7000	11 000
Payments/cash out	8000	12 000	12 000	6000	8000
Bank balance c/f	5000	3000	−1000	1000	3000

This cash flow forecast shows that the business may have a deficit in March but that it should only last one month. The owner or manager could then either try to improve his cash receipts to avoid this or seek an overdraft from the bank. He would be able to show the manager that he predicted that the difficulty would only last one month.

- Most businesses would use a computer spreadsheet program to enable them to track their cash flow. This would make the forecast easy to update.

- A cash flow forecast is usually expected to be included within a business plan for a new business. The bank manager or anybody providing capital to help set up the business would check that the predictions in the cash flow forecast were realistic. They would also try to spot any likely future problems.

- A cash flow forecast can also be shown as a graph so that it is easy to compare the forecast with the actual cash flow.

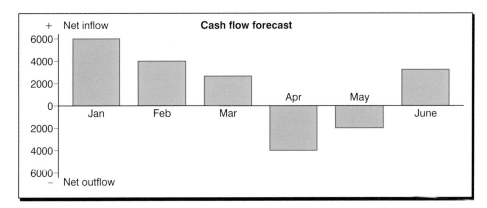

- In this cash flow forecast the business is predicted to have a surplus in January, February and March but this will be quickly used up in April. April and May both have a predicted deficit but the situation is expected to improve in June.

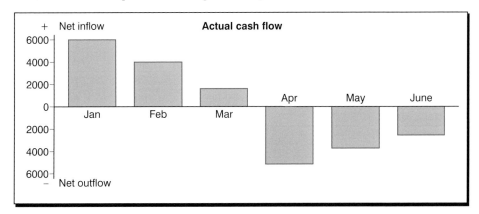

- In this actual cash flow we can see that the business did not have as many inflows as predicted in March and was still showing a deficit in June. Because the owner did not predict the deficit in June he may have run into difficulties, for example by not organising his bank overdraft for long enough.

Cash flow forecasts

1 Match the following terms with their definitions. (4)

Cash inflow	Flow of money out of the business
Cash outflow	Inflows are greater than outflows
Cash surplus	Inflows are smaller than outflows
Cash deficit	Flow of money into the business

2 What is a cash flow forecast? (3)

3 Explain how producing a cash flow forecast can help a business? (3)

4 Copy and complete this cash flow forecast table. (7)

	Jan	Feb	Mar	Apr
Bank balance b/f	2000		4000	−1000
Cash receipts	12 000	10 000	8000	8000
Total cash in		16 000	12 000	
Payments/cash out	8000	12 000		8000
Bank balance c/f			−1000	

5 Explain what the above cash flow forecast shows. (3)

The answers are on page 112.

- The usual objective for any business is to make a **profit**. That means the business will have more money coming in (**sales revenue**) than money going out (**expenditure**).

- A **profit and loss account** is produced by the business to show details of how the profit has been made in the past year. This information is used by the business to compare against previous years and other similar businesses. Stakeholders in the business such as banks, shareholders and employees will all be interested in seeing how the business has performed. Public limited companies must publish their accounts by law.

- There are two types of profit: **gross profit** and **net profit**.

  Gross profit = Sales revenue – Cost of sales

  Net profit = Gross profit – Expenses

- **Cost of sales** is the value of the stock of goods that has been sold. In examinations you are usually given this figure but you may have to work it out.

  Cost of sales = Opening stock + Purchases – Closing stock

- **Expenses** are the costs involved in running the business such as wages, advertising and electricity.

Case study

Sally's Ice Cream Parlour

Sales revenue = £10 000
Cost of sales = £2000
Expenses = £4000

Gross profit = Sales revenue – Cost of sales
= £10 000 – £2000
= £8000

Net profit = Gross profit – Expenses
= £8000 – £4000
= £4000

Profitability ratios

● In order to decide how well a business is performing it is useful to be able compare the ratios of net or gross profit to sales revenue. This makes it easier to compare different years' performance or the performance of different companies.

● **Gross profit to sales revenue ratio** shows the proportion of a business's sales revenue that is gross profit. It can be worked out as a % or a ratio.

Case study

Sally's Ice Cream Parlour

Gross profit   = £8000
Net profit   = £4000
Sales revenue = £10 000

$$\text{Gross profit to sales revenue ratio} = \frac{\text{Gross profit} \times 100\%}{\text{Sales revenue}}$$

$$= \frac{8000 \times 100\%}{10\,000}$$

$$= 80\%$$

or

Gross profit : Sales revenue = 8000 : 10 000

$$= 8 : 10$$

$$= 4 : 5$$

Remember to show all your working because if you do make a simple mistake you will then only lose one mark out of possibly five or more marks.

- **Net profit to sales revenue ratio** shows the proportion of sales revenue that is net profit. This is the return that the business is getting from the sales it is making.

- A higher ratio from one year to the next shows that the business is more profitable.

Case study

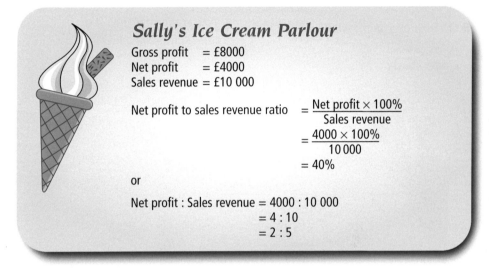

Sally's Ice Cream Parlour

Gross profit   = £8000
Net profit   = £4000
Sales revenue = £10 000

$$\text{Net profit to sales revenue ratio} = \frac{\text{Net profit} \times 100\%}{\text{Sales revenue}}$$

$$= \frac{4000 \times 100\%}{10\,000}$$

$$= 40\%$$

or

Net profit : Sales revenue = 4000 : 10 000

$$= 4 : 10$$

$$= 2 : 5$$

- If a business wants to improve its profitability it needs to reduce either the cost of sales or its expenses. If a business increases its sales revenue it does not necessarily increase its profits.

- **Return on capital employed (ROCE)** shows how much net profit the business is making in proportion to the amount of capital invested into the business.

- A high return on capital employed shows that the investment into the business was worthwhile. It can be compared with other companies, previous years or the amount of return the owners could have obtained by putting their money into a bank savings account.

- *Return on capital employed (ROCE)* $= \dfrac{Net\ profit \times 100\%}{Total\ capital\ employed}$

Case study

Sally's Ice Cream Parlour

Year 1
Net profit = £4000
Capital employed = £32 000

$$ROCE = \frac{Net\ profit \times 100\%}{Total\ capital\ employed}$$
$$= \frac{4000 \times 100\%}{32\,000}$$
$$= \frac{400\%}{32}$$
$$= 12.5\%$$

This shows that for every £100 invested into the business a profit of £12.50 is being made.

Year 2
Net profit = £6000

$$ROCE = \frac{Net\ profit \times 100\%}{Total\ capital\ employed}$$
$$= \frac{6000 \times 100\%}{32\,000}$$
$$= \frac{600\%}{32}$$
$$= 18.75\%$$

Therefore the return on capital employed has improved.

Balance sheet

- The balance sheet shows what the business is worth on a particular date.

- It has three main parts:
  - **Capital** is the money invested into the business.
  - **Assets** are everything that the business owns and has a value.
  - **Liabilities** are all the debts of the business.

- The balance sheet shows the stakeholders how well the firm is performing at any one time and can be compared with previous years and that of other companies.

- There are certain key terms associated with balance sheets that you should know.
  - **Fixed assets** are things the business owns that are used for production or are likely to be used for more than one financial year.
  - **Current assets** are things that are cash or easily turned into cash such as stock of goods, money owed by debtors or money in the bank account
  - **Current liabilities** are debts owed to others that must be paid by the business within the year. They include creditors who have supplied goods to the business but have not yet been paid for them.
  - **Retained profits** are profits made by the business in the previous year that have been kept within the business, possibly to help it expand.
  - **Capital employed** is all the money put into the business and so includes original money invested by the owners, retained profit and money lent to the business in the long term.

- Capital which is part of the information needed for calculating the return on capital employed could be given in the form of the balance sheet figure for capital employed.

Liquidity ratios

- Liquidity ratios look at the ability of the business to pay its debts. Assets that are easily turned into cash such as money in the bank are said to be **liquid**.

- Information needed to calculate liquidity ratios is contained in the balance sheet.

- The two ratios that you need to know are the **current ratio** and the **acid test**.

- The formula for current ratio is *current assets: current liabilities*. This ratio should normally be approximately 1.5 : 1.
  Too high a ratio and money could be better used by the business.

- The formula for acid test is *(current assets – stock) : current liabilities*. This ratio should normally be between 0.5 : 1 and 1 : 1 for the business to be safe from bankruptcy. Stock is deducted from the current assets as it may take too long to dispose of.

Case study

Sally's Ice Cream Parlour

Cash   = £200
Stock   = £2500
Bank   = £1800
Debtors   = £500
Current liabilities = £2500

Current ratio = Current assets : Current liabilities
Current assets = Stock + Debtors + Bank + Cash
                = £(2500 + 500 + 1800 + 200)
                = £5000
Current liabilities = £2500
Current ratio   = 5000 : 2500
                  = 2 : 1

Acid test = (Current assets – Stock) : Current liabilities
          = (5000 – 2500) : 2500
          = 2500 : 2500
          = 1 : 1

Business finance

1 Who would be interested in looking at the profit and loss account of a business? (1)

2 What is meant by cost of sales? (1)

3 If sales revenue is £12 000, cost of sales is £6000 and expenses are £3000, calculate the net profit.
Show all your workings. (5)

4 Calculate the gross profit : sales revenue ratio if sales revenue is £12 000 and the gross profit is £8000. (4)

5 What is the formula for return on capital employed? (3)

6 What are the three main parts of a balance sheet? (3)

7 Why are liquidity ratios important? (1)

8 What should the current ratio be approximately? (1)

9 What is taken away from the current assets when calculating the acid test? (1)

The answers are on page 113.

- Market research is essential because a business needs to know as much as it can about its potential customers in order to reduce the risk of producing or selling the wrong goods. It also needs to know the best price to charge, how to sell the goods and where to advertise them.

- A business that aims at a small market segment, such as a sports shop that specialises in water polo, is said to exploit a **niche market**.

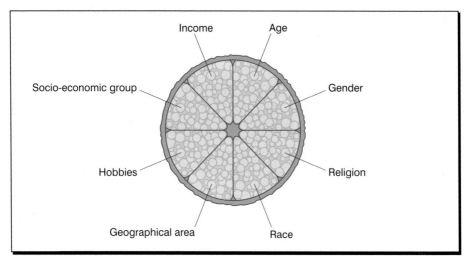

Market segments

- A business may analyse its own **s**trengths, **w**eaknesses, **o**pportunities and **t**hreats. This is called a **SWOT analysis** to find the position in the market of its products.

Methods of researching the market

- There are two methods of gaining information about potential consumers:
  - **desk research**
  - **field research**.

Desk research

- Desk research uses information that has already been found out by someone else. This information is called **secondary data**.

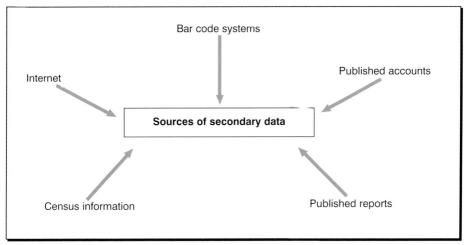

- The main disadvantages of desk research are:
  - Information can be out of date by the time it is available to be used.
  - The information may not be exactly what the business needs to know because it was collected for another purpose.
  - The information may not be accurate.
  - The information could be very expensive to obtain.

- The advantages of desk research are:
  - The information is collected on a larger scale than a small business could manage.
  - A lot of time can be saved by not having to go out and collect information from individuals.

Field research

● Field research uses information that the business finds out itself from consumers. This information is called **primary data**.

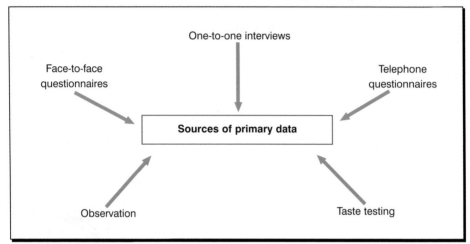

● The main disadvantages of field research are:
   ■ Money can easily be wasted unless the right segment of the market is questioned.
   ■ The questions must be asked very carefully or the answers may not be valid.
   ■ Results can be hard to analyse, for example if too many **open questions** are used. Open questions have no choices of answer to pick from.
   ■ For the research to be valid, the number of people questioned needs to be significant. This can be very expensive.

● The advantages of field research are:
   ■ The information is up to date.
   ■ The information is specific to the business.

Sampling

- A business can only ask a small proportion of the whole target market it is aiming at. Sampling is a method of choosing those who should be asked.

- A **random sample** is where a percentage of the market is approached, with everyone having an equal chance of being asked.

- A **quota sample** is where a specified number of each market segment is chosen according to the number of people in each segment.

- A **targeted sample** is where a particular group of consumers is chosen and only those people asked.

Analysing the results

- **Qualitative information** is information that is given in depth to the questions asked. The information can be very useful but is often descriptive and cannot be shown by a graph or easily analysed.

- **Quantitative information** contains results that are easily added up and can be shown on a graph and analysed.

- Always be careful how you interpret market research findings. Just because something is on a graph does not make it true!

- In a pre-issued case study you may be given information that is deliberately unhelpful to the business. If you spot this, try to refer to the quality of the information given. For example, you may be told that a business asked ten people if they would buy CDs before setting up the business of a music shop. You should point out that the sample was too small to be significant.

Market research

1 What are the main reasons for conducting market research? (2)

2 Match the following terms:

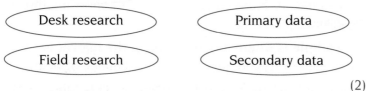

Desk research   Primary data

Field research   Secondary data

(2)

3 What method of research and type of information is obtained by using the Internet? (2)

4 What type of data may be out of date or not exactly what the business needs? (1)

5 Give four possible factors that a business must take into account when conducting primary research. (4)

6 Complete this sentence.
Questionnaires and observations are methods of obtaining _____ data. (1)

7 Complete this sentence.
'What sort of cheese do you like?' is an example of an _____ question. (1)

8 Explain the difference between qualitative and quantitative information. (4)

9 Name three types of sampling methods. (3)

The answers are on page 114.

- The **marketing mix** is the combination of a number of elements often called the '**four Ps**'.
  - Product
  - Price
  - Promotion
  - Place

- Decisions need to be made about all the four Ps so that the business can trade. A marketing strategy is a combination of the four Ps that can be used together to help the business achieve its objectives.

The product

- The product can be either goods or services.

- Large businesses will often have a range of products and this is one way that businesses can expand.

- Where a business chooses to add different products to its product range this is known as **diversification**. Diversification reduces the risk a business faces because it does not depend on one product that may, for example, go out of fashion.

- **Branding** is the unique way in which products are known. It can be a name, a logo or something as simple as a set of colours.

- Businesses protect their brands by using **trade marks**. This is a legal system of registering the brand name.

- Some brands are so successful that their name becomes the generic name for a group of products. For instance, a hoover is not always associated with the Hoover brand.

- Some products, such as farm produce, cannot easily be branded although producers increasingly try to do so by growing a unique variety of, say, apples.

Price

- There are a large number of factors that a business takes into account when setting a price for its products. These include:
  - how much the product costs to make
  - the results of market research conducted to find out how consumers are likely to react to a price
  - what competitors are charging.

- In economic theory, price should be the **equilibrium point** where the quantity **supplied** by the business equals the quantity **demanded** by the consumer. However, in real life, businesses do not have sufficiently accurate information to draw up the supply or demand curves.

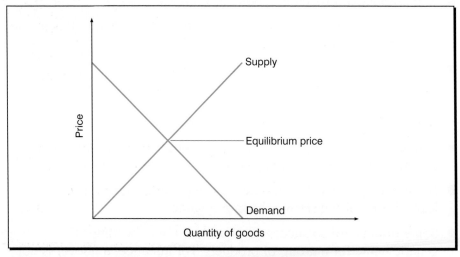

Typical supply and demand curve

- **Cost-plus pricing** is a very simple form of pricing which does not take into account the views of the consumer. All the costs involved in making the product are added up and then a **mark-up** is added onto the cost to give the profit. The mark-up will vary between different types of business.

- **Competitor-based pricing** chooses a price very similar to that of the business's competitors. This is used for similar products and the businesses have to use **non-price competition** to try and sell their goods. Examples of non-price competition include a free gift with purchase or free delivery.

- **Penetration pricing** means charging a low price for a product to get it established on the market. By charging a lower price than its competitors, the business hopes to get a share of the market. When the product is established the business may then raise the price so that it can make more of a profit. The main disadvantage is that this method of pricing can lead to a **price war** in which all the competitors lower their prices.

- **Creaming** or **skimming** is often used for innovative products when they are first introduced onto the market. A high price is charged and the product is often seen as a luxury. After a while the price is lowered so that more people can buy it. The high price can either make a lot of profit for the business or help cover high costs of developing the new product.

- **Loss leaders** are products that are sold at cost or below their cost price to attract people to the business. It is hoped that the consumers will buy not only the product that is being sold at this price but also other products at normal prices. For example, a supermarket may sell baked beans at 6p a can to encourage customers into a store. They hope and expect that people will also buy bread to make the toast to go with the baked beans.

- **Price discrimination** is a method of selling the same product at a range of different prices to suit different consumers. The different consumers may be kept separate by where they live, or by introducing rules such as when the goods must be ordered by or what age the consumer is. For example, pre-booked cinema tickets may be cheaper or the same seat may cost less if you are under 16.

Promotion

- **Promotion** informs potential consumers about the product and attempts to persuade them to purchase it. It is more than advertising, it includes **public relations activities** such as customer relations, sponsorship, free samples and competitions.

- **Advertising** can simply inform the public that a product is now available or it can try and persuade them that the product is new and exciting and should be bought NOW!

- The Advertising Standards Authority control advertising. All advertisements must be 'legal, decent, honest and truthful'.

Collins must not make any false claims about their revision books. For example, they cannot say, 'Buy this book (don't read it!) and you are guaranteed an A grade'.

- Some products such as milk are advertised **generically**. 'The White Stuff' campaign on behalf of the whole dairy industry has been produced to persuade people to drink more milk generally.

Advertising media

- **Television advertising** is very expensive – in excess of £1000 per minute – but is very effective in reaching potential consumers. It can be easily targeted to reach different market segments, for example, people interested in gardening or sport.

- **Radio advertising** is also effective at reaching certain market segments based upon age or interest. It is cheaper than television, costing from about £600 per minute. However, it is often harder to remember a lot of facts from just hearing an advertisement so they are often repeated many times.

- **Newspaper and magazine advertisements** vary in cost according to how many copies of the publication are circulated. Some magazines are published monthly and are more likely to be re-read than a daily newspaper. Targeting particular segments is easy as there are magazines published that are aimed at most market segments.

- **Posters and billboards** can be part of a national campaign or can be used in a specific locality. Other than this it can be hard to reach a particular target market. Local newspapers often advertise their main stories this way outside newsagents. The message has to be short and 'catchy' as only a little information can be taken in by passers-by this way.

- **Direct mail** can be targeted and involves directly contacting likely customers. It is not just a way of advertising, it is a way of selling that does not use wholesalers and retailers. It can only be as effective as the list of likely customers that the business is able to use.

Other methods of promotion

- **Customer relations** involves:
  - customer care, making sure that the customer is treated correctly at all times
  - handling complaints quickly
  - allowing goods to be exchanged if the customer has a change of mind.

  These all help a business to build a good reputation and encourage repeat business.

- **Sponsorship** is an increasingly popular method of promotion and includes sponsorship of television programmes such as the weather forecast. It can be very effective but very expensive. It is also popular for businesses to have deals with football teams and other sporting activities.

- **Samples** are sometimes given away inside supermarkets and can be an effective way to encourage consumers to try a new product. They can also be delivered to homes and some types of product can be included in magazines. Individual samples may be expensive to hand out or have to be specifically produced.

The name of the football team's sponsor features clearly on their shirts.

Place

- In the context of the marketing mix, place means how the product is sold to the customer, that is, the **channel of distribution** from the producer to the customer.

- The usual channels of distribution include:

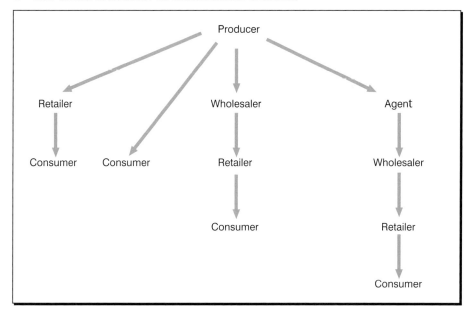

- Each channel will expect to make a profit from handling the goods.

- A **wholesaler** buys products in bulk from the **producer** and sells them on in smaller quantities to **retailers**. This is known as breaking bulk.

- The channels of distribution used depend on the nature of the product. Individually designed products are usually sold direct to the consumer. Products that are made on a large scale and sold individually will usually be distributed through a wholesaler. Large stores and supermarkets often buy direct from the producer and miss out the wholesaler.

Deciding on the marketing mix

- A business can choose to use a **marketing agency** to handle the whole marketing mix. This can be useful for a business that does not have a specific person skilled in marketing.

- The marketing strategy must be considered as a whole. If a business chooses to price their goods at a high price so that they are seen as luxury products then the advertising should reinforce this idea.

Packaging

- **Packaging** is often included in the marketing mix as the fifth 'P'.

- Packaging helps reinforce the product's image of being a luxury or everyday product.

- Even simple things like colours can be important when choosing the packaging. It is unlikely that milk would be sold in brown cartons or bottles as it would not look clean or fresh.

- Perfume is often sold in elaborate packaging to give the effect of luxury.

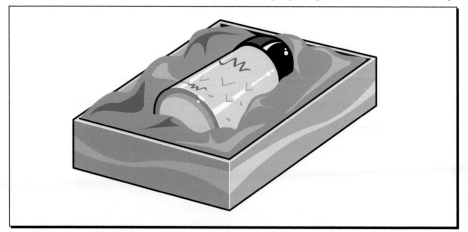

Marketing mix

1 Explain what is meant by the term marketing strategy? (3)

2 Complete this sentence.

A farm opening up part of the house for bed and breakfast is an example of _____. (1)

3 How can businesses protect their brands? (1)

4 Match each of these costs with its meaning. (4)

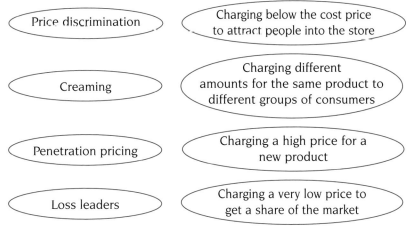

Price discrimination

Charging below the cost price to attract people into the store

Creaming

Charging different amounts for the same product to different groups of consumers

Penetration pricing

Charging a high price for a new product

Loss leaders

Charging a very low price to get a share of the market

5 Which organisation ensures that advertisements do not break the law? (1)

6 'A generically advertised product is one in which individual producers produce different advertisements.'

True or false? (1)

7 Describe two main advantages of advertising in a monthly magazine. (2)

8 What is the main disadvantage of television advertising. (1)

9 Describe three ways a business can provide good customer relations. (3)

10 What does a wholesaler do? (2)

11 Which is the most direct channel of distribution? (1)

The answers are on page 115.

- All products have a natural progression that includes **launch, growth, maturity, saturation** and **decline**. This is known as the **product life cycle**.

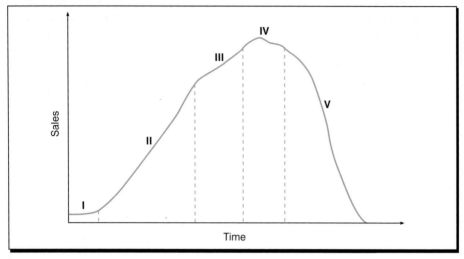

A *typical product life cycle*

These stages are shown on the graph above.

I The launch of a product is when it is newly introduced onto the market. At this stage the sales will be very low and the costs to the business very high.

II This period of rapid growth follows, the product becomes established and starts to achieve a share of the market.

III At maturity the product is enjoying high sales but they are not growing rapidly. There may be copies of the product coming onto the market.

IV At this stage the market is saturated, with either most customers already owning the product or many copies of the original product for sale.

V At the final stage in the product life cycle the sales are declining rapidly until it is no longer worth continuing to produce the product.

- Not all products however will follow the exact path described on page 66. Some products may prove very unsuccessful and disappear from the market after their launch.

- A business may decide to try to prevent the decline in sales of their products and introduce **extension strategies** to boost sales and appeal to new customers. These may include bringing out variants to the product such as a different flavour or changing the packaging.

- The diagram below shows what would happen to the product life cycle if extension strategies were successful.

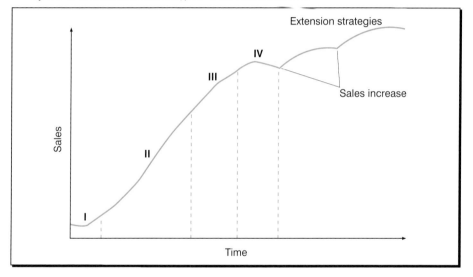

- Product development does not only happen before the launch of the product onto the market but also takes place when the product is approaching decline.

- By using extension strategies, a business can help to maintain its market share without having to introduce a completely new product with high development costs.

Product life cycle

1 Draw and fully label a graph showing the five stages of a product life cycle. (10)

2 Place the following products in their appropriate stage of the product life cycle:

Cassette players, DVD players, organic food, CDs, hair dryers (5)

Launch	Growth	Maturity	Saturation	Decline

3 How might a business attempt to halt the decline in sales of a product? (1)

4 At what stages in the life of a product might product development take place? (2)

5 Suggest ways in which a producer of children's sweets might try to extend their product life cycle. (2)

The answers are on page 116.

- Production is the process whereby goods or services are created to satisfy the needs of the public.

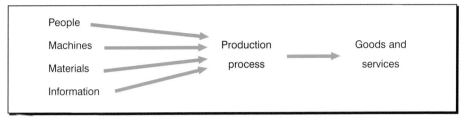

- Production is divided into three stages:
  - Primary production
  - Secondary production
  - Tertiary production

Primary production

- **Primary production** is the process of extracting raw materials, for example, farming or mining.

- Nothing is done to add value to the raw materials.

Secondary production

- **Secondary production** is concerned with the making of the goods.

- This is where value is added to the raw materials, for example milk is processed into cheese.

Tertiary production

- **Tertiary production** is the provision of services.

- Examples of tertiary production are hotels, banking services and cinemas.

Methods of production

- There are three main methods of production that you will need to be able to discuss in the examination:
  - Job production
  - Batch production
  - Flow production.

Job production

- Job production means that goods or services are produced individually to meet specific customer needs. These could include a bridge or tunnel, a unique wedding dress or a service such as a hair cut.

A *unique product*

- An advantage of job production is that each item can be different. This can create high quality goods or services that can be sold at a high price.

- In job production skilled labour is often used to produce the goods. Workers tend to be highly motivated and this also leads to high quality goods being produced.

- A disadvantage is that production can be very slow as it is hard to speed up the process if each item is different. This makes the costs of production high.

- Another disadvantage is that a lot of workers are needed which leads to high wages costs.

Batch production

- In batch production a set number of one product is made before production is stopped and another set of products is made. Often one process is completed at a time before the product moves onto the next part of the process. An example is the making of bread rolls, where a quantity of dough is made. It is then left to rise, after this it is shaped into rolls and again left to rise. The rolls are then baked and cooled.

- Other examples of batch production are books, clothing and jam.

- The advantages of batch production over job production are that costs per unit may be less as less labour is used and production can be quicker. It is more likely that specialised machinery can be used.

- Disadvantages of batch production are that goods may need to be stored so this increases costs. Also tasks become more routine and therefore workers may be less motivated than in job production.

Flow production

- In flow production goods are made continuously without stopping the production line. Often a conveyor belt is used to move goods along the production line and the process is automated. Goods are produced at a constant rate and quality.

- One of the main advantages of mass production is the large **output**, that is, the quantity of goods that can be produced. This results in low costs per unit produced and the business can usually benefit from **economies of scale**. Economies of scale mean that unit costs are lower as the business produces more goods.

- A disadvantage of flow production is that there can be a huge cost involved in setting up the production line. Once set up, it is often difficult to change the product so there is less flexibility. Workers are harder to motivate in this type of production because the tasks involved tend to be unskilled and repetitive.

- Products made by flow production include cans of baked beans, pots of yoghurt and also cars.

These robots are transporting car bodies to the next stage of production. They are part of an automated flow system used in car manufacturing.

Stock control

- **Lean production** is the production of goods in the most efficient way possible to ensure that there is no waste. All resources are used in the best way possible to reduce costs.

- An important part of lean production is **JIT** (Just in time), which is concerned with the supply of the stock needed for production. Detailed planning is needed and a good relationship between suppliers and the business must be built up so that stock is received just before it is needed on the production line, possibly as little as 30 minutes before it is used.

- Lean production also maximises the use of flexible and multi-skilled workforces, using workers where they are most needed at any one time so that they can achieve the best performance.

- **Kanban** is an approach to production that uses JIT stock control and leads to stock being pulled into the production line only when it is needed.

- Any strategy that involves JIT depends on constantly high quality goods being supplied. Production can be delayed by transport problems. Changing suppliers can also cause problems, as trust between the businesses is very important.

- Too much stock held by a business means that too much capital is tied up which could be used more efficiently. Also, the stock needs to be stored, thus using up land, buildings and labour to ensure that is secure. If it is kept for too long, stock can deteriorate, for example wood may warp or rot.

Efficiency

- Efficiency means making the best possible use of the resources of production, that is, getting the best output from the inputs.

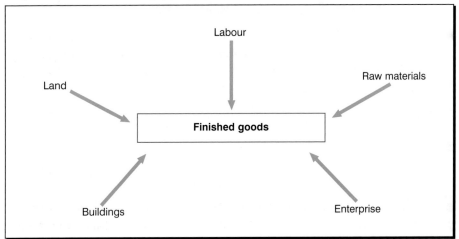

Methods of measuring efficiency

- **Productivity** is a measure of the amount of goods produced over a period of time, per machine or per worker. This can be compared between different periods of time or it can be compared between different businesses. The amount produced can be compared with the **capacity**, which is the maximum that could be produced with the given resources.

- **Unit cost** is calculated as the cost of producing one unit of the product. It is worked out by dividing the total costs by the amount of goods produced.

- **Product quality** is usually measured by testing a sample of the goods produced for faults.

- **Down time** or **idle resources**, when either one of the resources or perhaps the whole factory is not being used, can be compared between years or different businesses.

Use of technology

- **CAD**, **computer-aided design**, uses computers to produce the design for the product so that problems can be solved before manufacture. CAD can suggest the most efficient use of raw materials so that there is a minimum amount of waste.

- **CAM**, **computer-aided manufacture**, uses computers to control the machinery producing the goods. This can increase the speed in which goods are produced and result in fewer errors.

- With both CAD and CAM the costs of the new technology have to be compared with the benefits of greater efficiency. The effect on the labour force and social costs and benefits also needs to be considered.

Investing in new technology

- Before investing in CAD or CAM technology the business will need to consider these questions.
  - What image does the business wish to have? Does it want to be known as up-to-date or retaining traditional values?
  - Will the business need to keep updating the technology, which may have ever-increasing costs?
  - Can the business obtain the necessary finance? Perhaps the money could be better spent on other developments.

- If you are studying Design and Technology it is worth checking your notes on this topic.

Production methods

1 Match the following terms with their meaning: (3)

(Tertiary production)　　(The extraction of raw materials)

(Primary production)　　(Manufacturing goods)

(Secondary production)　　(Providing services)

2 Complete the table showing the most likely method of production for the following products. (4)

Product	Job, batch or flow production
Wedding dress	
Size 10 jeans	
Designing a new website	
Golf balls	

3 Complete this sentence.

The key objective of lean production is to ensure that there is no _____. (1)

4 Name the system of stock control used in lean production. (1)

5 List the three main disadvantages of flow production. (3)

6 Complete this sentence.

The method of stock being pulled through the production line is known as _____. (1)

7 How can productivity be measured? (3)

8 Explain two ways in which CAM could benefit a business? (2)

9 What is 'down time'? (1)

10 Complete this sentence.

Before deciding to implement CAD or CAM the business needs to weigh up the costs against the likely _____. (1)

The answers are on page 117.

- Quality control is not about producing the best possible goods, it is about ensuring that the goods are produced to a standard that is expected and that they are fit for the purpose for which they are intended.

- Many businesses do not have quality as their main objective; low price can be more important and for some goods such as fashion items, appearance is more important.

- Quality can often be improved by a variety of methods but the business has to weigh up the costs of improving the quality against the benefits of likely increased sales and reputation.

- The business needs to consider the legal requirements. For example, the weight of goods needs to be as given on the packet. Also, the manufacture of the goods must not result in them being dangerous to use, such as having an electrical fault.

- The costs of having poor quality can be prosecution if legal requirements are not followed, a bad reputation and falling sales.

Managing quality

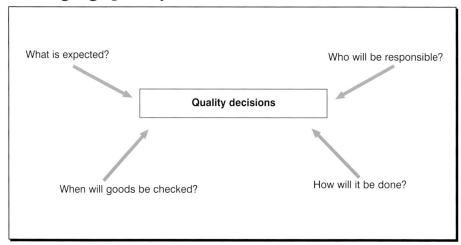

Traditional methods of managing quality

- Quality control is a traditional method of checking goods to ensure that the desired quality is produced. There may be a person whose specific job is to check finished goods to ensure that they meet the required standard.

- As an example of traditional quality control, suppose the product is a CD. The quality controller might have a list of points to check such as:
  - the CD case must be scratch free
  - the insert correctly folded and not creased
  - the CD printed correctly, etc.

  One in every 1000 CDs may be played and checked for sound quality.

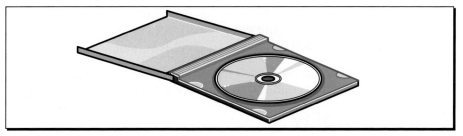

- Traditional quality controllers can also check the raw materials and the goods at the end of each stage of production. This system is known as **quality assurance**.

- Faults found, either at the end of the whole manufacturing process or at the end of a stage in the process, can be expensive because the whole batch can be wasted. In some instances, the products can be re-made so the waste is mainly in the time used but this is not always the case.

Modern methods of managing quality

- **Statistical process control** is a method whereby the machine operators take some responsibility for checking the quality of the goods they produce by checking their machines at regular intervals. By not leaving all the checking to the end of the process less waste is produced. Also costs are reduced because fewer specialist quality controllers are employed.

- **Kaizen** is the Japanese method of continuous improvement. Everybody in the company is encouraged to make suggestions as to how the production process and the quality of the product can be improved. By using the principles of Kaizen it is hoped to prevent problems, rather than wasting resources by finding faults after goods have been manufactured.

- **Quality circles** are a method of improving quality by having discussion groups of all levels of workers who meet together to identify problems and suggest solutions. The underlying principle is that the workers on the shop floor understand the problem best and also may know the solution. By encouraging them to contribute their ideas, the workers are likely to be motivated as it is a form of **job enrichment**.

- **Total quality management (TQM)** is another Japanese method of managing quality by involving everybody in the business organisation, not just in the production department. Quality is 'everybody's business' and there is an underlying principle of 'right first time'. Usually each group of workers views each other as a customer resulting in more care being taken. TQM can eliminate the need to test products at the end of the manufacturing process and usually includes quality circles and Kaizen.

- The benefit of TQM is that costs are reduced, by eliminating waste, and this should outweigh the costs of training people to operate the system. Fewer rejects should improve the reputation of the business and lead to increased sales.

- **Benchmarking** is the process of comparing the products produced against those of the most efficient producer. This means that a business does not just consider its own production methods but tries to understand its competitors' methods. The obvious difficulty with this is obtaining information from competitors.

Quality control

1 Explain why a business might not have quality as its primary objective. (4)

2 Suggest two ways the law might affect the quality of goods a manufacturer chooses to produce. (2)

3 Explain the disadvantages to a business of not aiming for a sufficient level of quality. (6)

4 Describe the usual methods used in traditional methods of managing quality to ensure that faulty goods do not reach the consumer. (2)

5 How could a business reduce the costs of faults if they are found at the end of the manufacturing process? (1)

6 Match the following quality management methods with their main feature. (4)

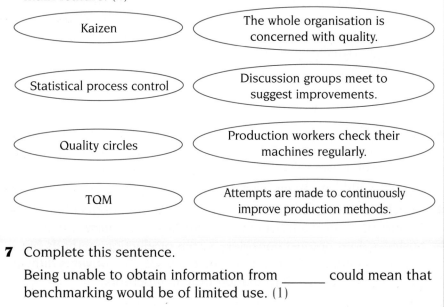

Kaizen	The whole organisation is concerned with quality.
Statistical process control	Discussion groups meet to suggest improvements.
Quality circles	Production workers check their machines regularly.
TQM	Attempts are made to continuously improve production methods.

7 Complete this sentence.

Being unable to obtain information from _____ could mean that benchmarking would be of limited use. (1)

The answers are on page 118.

Factors affecting the choice of location

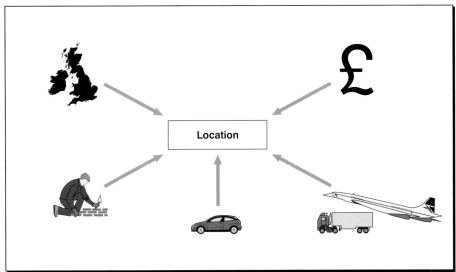

- Certain geographical features of the UK are important for businesses, for example the presence of water for cooling in the power industry and the climate for agriculture. Safety is another consideration so dangerous products are often not made in very heavily populated areas.

- The cost of the site is a key factor for many industries. A business will need to find out if the type and size of premises is available in their chosen location at a price they can afford to rent or buy. The cost to the business will be affected by the amount of support that local, national or EC government will provide. Grants may be made to cover all or part of the cost of premises in some areas.

- The availability of people, **labour**, to work in the business is important. Are there sufficient skilled workers available in the area? What are the wages that are expected by these people? Suitable training facilities are important too for some businesses.

- The **infrastructure** is important. This means that there are suitable communications facilities available – both transport and postal/delivery services. Other businesses that provide support should also be available such as those which perform routine maintenance for machinery. If the infrastructure is not there costs can rise considerably, for example products may need to be flown in at a much higher cost than road transport.

- The nature of the product, whether it is bulk reducing or bulk increasing will affect whether the production takes place near the raw materials or near the consumer. **Bulk reducing** means that a large amount of raw materials are needed to produce a small amount of finished goods. **Bulk-increasing** goods should be made near to customers, for example car production takes place near to large centres of population.

Inertia

- Some businesses were established in a certain area many years ago for sound reasons that are no longer relevant. These include industries located near to coalfields when coal was the main source of power available. Other businesses located by chance in an area because the founder had his home there, for example. If such businesses refuse to re-locate they are said to be suffering from inertia and may not be able to benefit from many advantages of certain other areas.

- There may also be some reluctance on the part of the owner(s) of small businesses to relocate to areas away from their family and friends. Although the market research might suggest that it is sensible to move, the owners may ignore this because of personal considerations.

Multinational organisations

- A **multinational** business is one that has its headquarters in one country but manufactures or operates in other countries. Such a business may concentrate part of its operations in one country, where perhaps labour costs are low, and use another country for basic assembly and as a retail base.

Advantages	Disadvantages
Provides jobs and income to an area.	Often away from home country. Provides unskilled jobs only.
Reduces the need for imports so improves the economy of the country.	Attempts to get round safety legislation, etc of their home country.
Improves skills within an area, e.g. provides up-to-date IT training that can be used by other businesses.	Can be a competitor for the local industry which may be more valuable to the area.
	Can try and influence the government against the best interests of the people.

Incentives to locate in an area

- Some countries within Europe and regions within the UK have higher unemployment than others. This has led to certain areas getting assistance from the government and being called **assisted areas** or **enterprise zones**. There is a wide variety of forms of assistance available, which changes regularly. These include advice and information and financial help in the form of grants or low interest loans. The presence of this help can persuade a business to locate in a particular area.

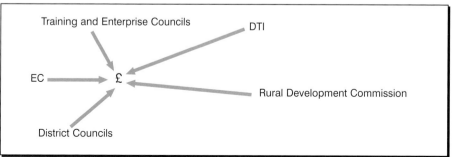

Location

1 Which of the following is not a factor affecting the choice of location? (1)

   A Availability of labour   **C** Job production

   B Price of property   **D** Infrastructure

2 Use an example to explain how climate could affect the location of a business. (3)

3 Match the factor affecting location with its example. (6)

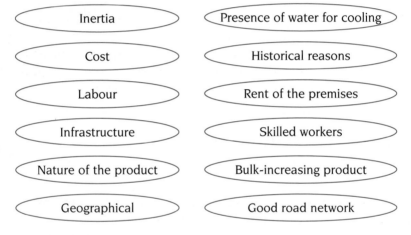

Inertia	Presence of water for cooling
Cost	Historical reasons
Labour	Rent of the premises
Infrastructure	Skilled workers
Nature of the product	Bulk-increasing product
Geographical	Good road network

4 Complete this sentence.

   A _____ is a business that operates in more than one country. (1)

5 Explain why the government may wish to encourage a business to locate in a specific area. (4)

6 Explain why a manufacturing business may need a good infrastructure. (4)

7 Which of the following is not a source of financial help to businesses seeking to locate in an area? (1)

   A Training and Enterprise Councils   **C** Inland Revenue

   B Rural Development Commission   **D** District Councils

The answers are on page 119.

- A business both has an effect on its external environment and is affected by it. The external influences on a business are:
  - Social
  - Legal
  - Economic
  - Environmental
  - Political
  - Technological.

Social influences

- Society and how it is made up affect business in many ways. One way is the **demographic** make up of the area, for example the age ranges of the inhabitants of the area would affect the market for entertainment. The main categories for analysing the demographic make-up of an area are:
  - age
  - social class
  - gender
  - income
  - region of residence.

- This table gives the usual socio-economic groupings used by businesses and government organisations.

Social grade	Occupation
Grade A	Top professional, e.g. lawyer
Grade B	Senior manager
Grade C1	Administrative or clerical
Grade C2	Skilled worker
Grade D	Semi or unskilled worker
Grade E	State dependent, e.g. unemployed

Legal influences

- The law affects businesses in many ways; there are laws governing all aspects of business activity. Most laws act as a **constraint** on business activity, that is, they prevent the business from doing something.

- Employment law covers two main areas:
  - Health and Safety
  - Equal opportunities.

Health and Safety

- **Health and Safety** laws cover both the workplace in general and specific industries such as mining.

- The main law is The Health and Safety at Work Act 1974. This stresses that the employer shares with the employee the responsibilities to keep the workplace a safe environment for all.

- Health and Safety laws increase costs to the employer by the need to provide training and special equipment. However, there will be savings in the reduction of time lost and compensation for injury. Also, the business's reputation will improve.

- Health and Safety training may be provided by trade unions as a benefit to their members.

- Health and Safety training may also be seen as staff development – a way of improving the skills of some workers. This could be a form of motivation.

Equal opportunities

- **Equal opportunities** means that all individuals have equal rights regardless of their:
  - gender
  - sexual orientation
  - age
  - physical characteristics
  - religion
  - racial group.

- There are not laws regarding all of these, for example employers can specify a particular age of employee that they wish to recruit.

- Equal opportunities legislation works in the interest of both the employer and employee because the best person for the job should be chosen. Some jobs have traditionally been done by a certain gender of worker and there can be a feeling that despite the statement on a job advertisement, indirect discrimination takes place. Equal opportunity is not the same as **positive discrimination** where there is a bias towards the characteristics previously discriminated against.

Protecting the consumer

- Businesses are also affected by laws protecting consumers from damaging their health or safety and from businesses exaggerating the qualities of their products. An example of such a law is the Food and Drugs Act 1955/1984, which states that it is illegal to sell goods that are 'unfit for human consumption'. It also protects consumers from businesses describing a product unfairly.

- There are also laws protecting the consumer that relate to accurate labelling of goods, including statements such as 'Contains 40% orange juice', and the country of origin for goods not produced in the UK.

Economic influences

- Changes in government policy can affect businesses. Fiscal policies are those that affect the way the government spends money and raises money through taxes. For example, the government can change the amount of money it spends on pensions, which will be good for businesses that make things that pensioners buy.

- Increasing taxes may affect the type of products that people buy. For example, high income tax might reduce the demand for luxury goods.

- Monetary policy is a way that the government tries to control the cost of borrowing money. Businesses are affected by monetary policy because it affects how much interest they have to pay on any money that they borrow. If interest rates are high then the business has to pay a lot of interest on any loans it has and so it may not be able to afford to borrow any more to expand or launch new products.

- If interest rates go down then consumers may be more likely to borrow money to buy luxury items like new cars.

Environmental influences

- Consumers have become more environmentally aware and this has led to businesses having to consider the environmental affects of their actions. Some of these effects are legislated against, for example pollution, and others are used by businesses for marketing purposes. Businesses will claim that their products are 'ozone friendly' or are packaged using recycled materials. Some of these actions will increase the costs to business; others will reduce costs and increase sales.

The symbol for recycled cardboard

Political influences

- Businesses can be affected by political factors such as **privatisation** of industry, that is returning industries that were run by the state to the private sector. Privatisation can also mean getting the local council to use private firms for some of its services or allowing private companies to run the bus routes.

- Those in favour of privatisation argue that a state monopoly can be just as harmful to the public as a private monopoly, causing inefficiency and high costs that the public have to pay for indirectly. Others argue that certain products and services are so important that they should not be left to private firms to charge whatever prices they think that they can.

Technological influences

- New technology has led to a growth in the use of computers within the service industries and improved production methods. This leads to greater efficiency for businesses and better quality products and services for the public. New technology calls for new skills from the workforce, which can mean more training and greater motivation.

- E-commerce has resulted in companies being able to reach a much larger market and to be 'open' 24 hours a day.

- The costs of new technology are, however, enormous and include the financial costs of purchasing the technology, its frequent upgrading and the effect on jobs. There are also Health and Safety concerns associated with new technology, for example for people who spend long days at a computer screen.

External costs and benefits

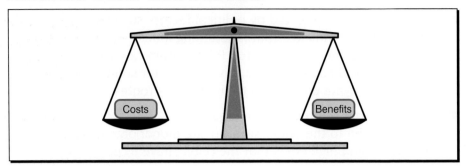

- When a business makes a decision regarding the production of goods or services, it creates external costs or benefits to the community. For example, if a business wishes to locate in an area, the local council will consider these costs and benefits before making a decision whether or not to support the development.

- External costs measure the cost to the whole of society of a business decision. These include pollution in the form of noise, smell or waste. Another external cost could be the loss of jobs caused by a business closure and the resultant loss of income.

- External benefits measure the benefit to the whole of society. These can include the regeneration of an area by more businesses moving into the area and extra spending from families where jobs have been created.

- It is quite difficult to put a monetary value on the external costs and benefits. A development in an area that improves the quality of life of its inhabitants, such as the provision of a youth club, is hard to put in money terms.

- Many developments have both external costs and benefits. For example, an old factory closing down will cause unemployment in the area but may remove a source of pollution.

- Pressure groups can try to cause sufficient publicity to prevent a business carrying out a proposed action that has many external costs. Sometimes opposing pressure groups can be involved in the arguments.

External environment

1 Complete this list.

The main external influences on a business are:

S_____

L_____

E_____

E_____

P_____

T_____ (6)

2 Complete this sentence.

Age and gender are examples of the _____ make-up of an area. (1)

3 State the two main areas covered by employment law. (2)

4 Who has the responsibility for ensuring that the workplace is a safe environment? (2)

5 Explain the two main ways in which consumers are protected by the law. (4)

6 Complete this sentence.

_____ policy is a means of controlling interest rates. (1)

7 How can the use of new technology motivate the workforce? (1)

8 Explain how e-commerce can increase the sales revenue of a business? (2)

9 Suggest an external benefit of an old mill closing down. (1)

The answers are on page 120.

Assessment objectives

- Assessment objectives are the qualities that are being tested in the GCSE examinations. They are the same for all examination boards.

- All four of these assessment objectives are given the same weighting of 25%.
  - **A** Demonstrate knowledge and understanding of the specified subject content.
    To get marks for this assessment objective you have to demonstrate your factual knowledge of business studies.
  - **B** Apply knowledge and understanding using appropriate terms, concepts, theories and methods effectively to address problems and issues.
    To get marks here you need to relate your factual knowledge to the business context given.
  - **C** Select, organise, interpret and use information from various sources to analyse problems and issues.
    To get marks for this objective you need to be able to choose figures from data given and then use them. This might include calculations or producing a table or a graph.
  - **D** Evaluate evidence, make reasoned judgements and present conclusions accurately and appropriately.
    To get marks for this objective you need to be able to form a conclusion and recommend a solution to a problem. To do this you may need to balance advantages and disadvantages.

Coursework issues

- Coursework accounts for 25% of the marks for most specifications and, if you are doing it, it is worth trying to maximise your marks. By the time you are using this revision guide, hopefully you will have completed most of your coursework, but there are still several points that you can check.

- Coursework has the same assessment objectives as described previously. Check your coursework for the following:
  - You have used several methods of obtaining information and said what they are, for example, interviews and conducting questionnaires. These should be properly carried out and in the case of questionnaires, you should have asked enough people.
  - You have selected and used information from several sources that you name. Don't just print out information and stick it in your folder – it must be used. If you use information from the Internet import it into a word processing file, making sure you say where it came from and how it helps you. If it is too late for you to do this now, write on your printouts where they are from and what they are for.
  - You have used business terms and concepts in your coursework. Don't just rewrite chunks from a text book. In many cases it is better to personalise statements, for example
  'If my business was a sole trader I would be able to make my own decisions...'
  rather than
  'A sole trader makes his own decisions...'
  - You have discussed advantages and disadvantages and made conclusions throughout your work, not just at the end.
  - Check your quality of written communication. Correct any spelling mistakes and check for any grammatical errors.

Before the examination

- Check that you know exactly how you will be examined. Make sure that you know the answers to the following questions:
  - Which examination board am I using?
  - How many examination papers will I take?
  - When are they?
  - How long is each examination?
  - Is a case study or several case studies used in the examination(s)? If so, is it pre-issued and when will I get it?

- Use past or specimen papers for revision. Make sure that you see the most recent ones available. Try to get hold of the mark scheme and make sure that you understand how your examination will be marked.

- Although it is very unlikely that exactly the same question will be asked on your examination paper as on a previous one, the style of the questions can be similar. Also, some topics can only really be asked about in one or two ways so they may be asked more often.

- Some examination boards like to begin their examination papers with fairly straightforward questions so that you settle into the examination and your nerves are calmed! Examiners want you to be able to show what you know and can do; they don't want everyone to do badly in their examination! This means it is worth looking back and seeing what has been asked in the past.

- Look again at the subject content in the specification for the syllabus you are taking. Examiners try and set questions covering as much of the subject content as possible. Do not try to 'topic spot'. Candidates sometimes try to ignore one section of the specification for example, finance, but they very rarely get away with it!

- Check you have the necessary equipment: blue or black pens, highlighter pen, pencils, a ruler and a calculator. Make sure that you take them to the examination room.

Command words

- Take care to read the command word in the question. It will be telling you how to get the marks available.

- Questions that ask for a decision, such as
  'Consider three methods of advertising and describe which would be best for Jackie' (15),
  do not have one correct answer. First you must discuss the advantages and disadvantages of each of the methods. Then you must make a choice and defend it – it would not normally matter which one you chose.

- 'Explain...' or 'Describe...' must never be answered with a list. You need to use phrases such as 'this means' in your answer and you need to expand or develop your answer. Often it is better to give just two or three points fully explained than lots of points with no detail.

- Questions that ask for evaluation need to be answered by either weighing up relevant factors or suggesting what needs to be done first and why. If it is in response to a case study, you should use the material in the case study to explain the best solution.

- A common type of question in an examination is:
  'Explain why Jackie should not advertise her business on television.' (12)

  A typical response might be:
  1. It is too expensive.
  2. It covers too wide an area.
  3. The advertisements are too short.

  Clearly this is not an explanation. It is a list and would not receive many marks.

  It would be much better to write short paragraphs on each point and not to list them. The same points could be used to write a much better answer:

  Television is a very expensive way of advertising costing thousands of pounds to produce the advertisements. This is the most important reason why Jackie should not use it. Usually only very large companies can afford to use this method. Other methods such as radio or newspapers could be used which would be much cheaper.

  For Jackie's business, television would cover too wide an area. Because she can only sell her goods in a small area it would be better to use a local form of advertisement, such as local paper or local radio.

  Jackie needs to give a lot of information about her products in her advertisements and television would not enable her to give enough detail. If she did it would be far too expensive. If she needs to give lots of details she would be better to have it printed in a leaflet, magazine or newspaper. This makes it much easier for customers to remember the information.

  This answer uses the same points but the candidate has explained them and would therefore get many more marks.

- The command word 'list' or 'what' can of course be answered in bullet points. In this case take careful note of how many marks there are available for this question and include that many points.

Pre-issued case studies

- The pre-issued case study forms a context for your examination. It is not intended that you use it to restrict your revision in any way.

- When you get the case study, first **highlight** any specific business studies terms and check that you understand their precise meaning.

- Read through the case study several times to ensure that you understand the English.

- Think about the type of business it is describing. Is it a partnership, a limited company, etc? How does this affect what the business can do?

- Having made a list of all the possible areas in the case study that suggest obvious questions, look again at the specification and the subject content. Think about how questions on each area could be asked. Revise each area of the subject content, not just the obvious areas.

- In the examination make sure that you relate your answer to the specific case study. The case study is pre-issued so that you use the specific context and you will lose a lot of marks if you do not do so.

In the examination

- Read carefully the instructions on the front of the paper.

- Follow the instructions on the examination papers very carefully. If you are sitting more than one paper, they could vary between the papers. On some examination papers you may be given a choice of questions, on others you must complete all the questions. If you are asked to answer three questions and you attempt four, the first three answers may be the only ones that are marked. Even if all four are marked (as some examinations boards will do) only the best three marks will be counted and you will have wasted valuable time.

- Look through the whole examination paper before you start answering any questions.

- Look at the number of marks in brackets after the examination question. This will tell you the maximum marks available for that question. You can use this to work out how long you can spend on each question. If the examination lasts one hour fifteen minutes and the total marks for the paper are 75 then, not allowing for reading time, you can only spend five minutes on a question worth 5 marks.

- You do not have to do the questions in the order they have been set, but the examiner has written them in an order that he/she thinks is logical. Sometimes the answer from one question can be used to answer the next. There is also a danger of you leaving out a question that you intended returning to, if you leave a question early on. If you do leave a question for later, check your paper carefully at the end.

- Try not to 'over answer' the early questions on the examination papers. This is the main reason why candidates run out of time. Often the first question is a straightforward one to settle you in the examination so do not get carried away and write too much. Look to see how many marks the answer is worth.

● Read the question very thoroughly before you start writing your answer. Check about halfway through that you are still answering the question and have not gone off the point.

● Check that you are answering the question from the correct viewpoint. For example,
'Explain how effective you think the Internet might be in reaching the type of people Jetwise want to recruit for a job vacancy' requires you to look at Internet use from the point of view of the business not the person applying for the job.

● Check also that you are making the correct comparisons. For example, in this question:
'Explain why David and Gwen might have chosen to become a partnership rather than a private limited company.'
many candidates compared a partnership to a sole trader or a plc. This meant that they got no marks despite understanding the advantages and disadvantages of a partnership.

● In each examination, 5% of the marks are available for quality of written communication. This can make a difference to your grade. Unless you are asked to do a calculation or provide a one-word answer, always write in full sentences. Try to use commas and paragraphs in longer answers. Check the spelling of any words used in the question or case study if one is given. It is worth reading through and looking for mistakes if you have time at the end of the examination.

● Do not answer any questions as a list unless you are specifically asked to do so in the question. Certainly you must not do this in any question that asks you to explain or describe anything. Often lists or unexplained points are harshly penalised. To make sure that you are not listing points, try to use 'joining words' between short sentences, such as 'and' or 'so'.

- If you are asked to draw a graph, perhaps for break even or a product life cycle, make sure that you label both the axes. **However accurate looking or beautifully drawn, a graph without axes labelled is meaningless and will get no marks.** A title is also helpful. Add any other labels that you can.

- In a calculation question always have a go and **show your working**. If you make a silly mistake then you will still get some marks. If you have no idea still try – you might pick up 1 or 2 marks for identifying the figures that should be used, even if you cannot remember the formula. If you are given figures in the stem of the question you can be pretty sure that those are the ones you are meant to be doing something with.

- Use any data you are given in the stem of the question. For example, in the question:
'Explain how well William's Café has performed in 2001'
you would need to use those figures given, and possibly calculate profitability ratios. You might have been given the figures for gross or net profit, or else had to calculate them in a previous question. If you know that you got them wrong in a previous question, carry on, you may still be able to get full marks for using them in the correct way.

- Try to use the appropriate business studies terms rather than general words, for example do not write 'money' when you mean 'profit' or 'sales revenue'. An aim of a business is to make profit not money.

- Try not to mix up words such as 'borrow' and 'lend'. A business may **borrow** money from a bank. The bank manager **lends** money to the business.

Non pre-issued case studies

- Many examination boards use case studies for their examination papers but these are not issued before the examination. Sometimes they are printed on a separate sheet from the examination paper. Other examination papers provide the stimulus of a case study and then ask a few questions followed by more of the same or a different case study. Whichever system your examination board uses, follow the instructions as given by the examiner. Always read the case study **before** you try to answer any questions.

- Follow the precise instructions given before answering the questions. For example, 'Read and use Data A to answer the following questions' means that you need to use the information in Data A of the case study and that it may well contain some hints to help you answer the question.

- If you are just given a case study with questions that follow, read through the whole case study to ensure that you understand it before answering any of the questions. Highlight key points in the case study.

- Some of the examination questions will require you to select information from the case study to answer the question. For other questions the case study may contain helpful clues.

- Make sure that you answer each question in context. Use the name of the business in your answer. Make sure that you use the context correctly. For example, if the business is a sole trader, check that your answer is applicable to a sole trader and not a limited company. For instance check that you have not suggested that he gets **more** shareholders to raise finance, when he would not have **any**.

- Maps or plans may be included in the case study to point you to specific problems or solutions. Use them – they are there for a purpose.

- In some examination papers information may be presented that is deliberately useless for you to spot and to criticise. For example, you may be told that a businessman has done a survey of ten people and proposes to base his business on this research. Do not be afraid to criticise the information you have been given.

Check yourself answers

1 OWNERSHIP AND CONTROL (PAGE 4)

1 The owners are responsible for all the debts of the business. (1) This means that they can lose all their own possessions if the business fails, (1) for example they may lose their home. (1) Always try and give at least one example to support your answer.

2 Sole proprietor. (1) Some examination boards use this term in their examination papers.

3 Sole trader. (1)
   Partnership. (1) These businesses have to be reformed if an owner dies.

4 Able to buy in bulk (1) so the unit cost is cheaper. (1) A larger business can buy their goods cheaper than a small business because of this.

5 A sole trader. (1) The owner will often have just a few workers who will have to do many tasks.

6 How much capital the partners will contribute. (1)
   How the profits will be shared. (1)
   The jobs each partner will do. (1)
   How the partnership will be ended. (1)

7 Private limited company (Ltd). (1)
   Public limited company (Plc). (1)

8 The shareholders. (1) These are people who have bought shares in the business.

9 The sole trader. (1)

10 Limited companies. (1)

11 The business exists in its own right. (1)

12 A limited company. (1) Both a private limited company and a public limited company have legal entity.

TOTAL

Check yourself answers

2 FORMS OF BUSINESS (PAGE 8)

1 A franchise is where a business has bought the right to trade under another company's name. (1) Be sure you know the correct terms: franchise, franchisee and franchiser.

2 **A** There is less risk because products are well known. (1)
  C The franchiser uses national advertising. (1)

3 Product development. (1)
  Marketing. (1)

4 Turnover is the total income from sales. (1) Do not confuse with profit.

5 Burger King. (1)
  McDonald's. (1)

6 Owners. (1)
  Workers. (1)
  Consumers. (1)

7 Because they are vital for the public. (1) There is a range of possible answers, such as because they need a lot of investment.

8 **B** BBC (1)
  D The Army (1)

9 Placing an organisation in the public sector. (1)

10 Encourages people to own shares. (1)
  Costs the government less. (1)
  Increases competition. (1)
  Increases efficiency. (1)
  Decisions made faster. (1)

TOTAL

1 Monopoly — A person with a financial interest in the business (1)

Merger — A business which controls a large part of the market (1)

Stakeholder — When businesses of a similar size join together (1)

2 Owners, managers, suppliers, customers, employees and creditors. (6) Try to use the correct business terminology. You can often get another mark for explaining the term, for example explaining what a creditor is.

3 Satisficing is being content to reach a particular level, (1) whereas maximising is making the most out of something. (1)

4 Survival. (1)
Profit. (1)
Growth. (1)
Survival will be an early objective. Once the business is more established it will aim for profit and growth.

5 To obtain reasonable pay so that they can support their family. (1)
To have good conditions of work so that they feel safe. (1)
There are many other reasonable answers. Where the question says 'explain', it is useful to use the words 'so that' in your answer.

6 A customer will want to pay low prices (1) whereas the business will want to make a lot of profit. (1) Again there are many other reasonable answers such as the customers will want high quality whereas the business will want to keep its costs down.

7 Internal. (1)
External. (1)

TOTAL

1 A letter of application (1)
   Complete an application form (1)
   Write a CV (1)
   Some businesses may ask for a letter of application and a CV
   or any combination of the three.
2 It is a curriculum vitae, an account of your life to date. (1)

3 A shortlist is a group of candidates invited for interview, (1)
   usually less than ten. (1)
4 The organisation may decide to give the applicants a test. (1)
   For example, they may use an aptitude test, (1) test mental
   arithmetic (1) or IT skills, (1) depending on the job. Remember
   the questions that ask you to describe are best answered by
   giving lots of examples. Look at the marks available as a guide
   to the length of the answer required.
5 Whether the right people would be likely to see the
   advertisement. (1)
   From how far away people would be interested in the job.(1)
   How much you can afford to spend. (1)
6 Who to contact (1)
   Job title (1)
   Pay being offered (1)
   Skills needed (1)
   There are other answers that could be given and would be
   marked correct such as any perks or how to apply for the job.
7 Pay (1)
   Hours of work (1)
   Job title (1)
   Again any reasonable answer would be accepted.

TOTAL

Check yourself answers

5 TRAINING (PAGE 19)

1. To explain dangers in the workplace (1) and to follow the law on Health and Safety (1).
2. Introducing new employees to the workplace. (1) This is nothing to do with selection and testing. It takes place after the worker has been appointed to their job.
3. **B** Increases output with the resources they have. (1) In the case of training, employers hope to increase the amount produced by training the workers.
4. So that employees know the aims and objectives of the company, (1) types of products made (1) and feel part of the company. (1) This helps them settle in faster and feel a valued member of the company. This makes them less likely to leave after only a short while.
5. Co-workers. (1)
   Supervisors. (1)
6. Canteen. (1)
   Fire exits. (1)
   Lockers. (1)
   You would include all the areas needed for the new worker's safety and comfort like toilets and places to smoke, eat, etc. The sooner the worker feels at home the sooner he will feel part of the company.
7. Off-the-job training (1)

8. It is cheaper, (1) more relevant to the job (1) and can use existing skilled workers to do it (1) so it can also motivate the people doing the training. (1)
9. It can motivate workers by showing that the business is interested in them (1) and can give them the chance to get qualifications (1) and possibly promotion. (1) If workers are motivated they are more likely to remain with the company.

TOTAL

1 They will work harder and be more efficient (1) and will be less likely to take time off work unnecessarily. (1) They will also be less likely to be late (1) and more likely to stay with the company for longer. (1)

2 More goods will be produced (1) and less money needs to be spent on recruitment. (1)

3 Self-actualisation   level 5 (1)
Status   level 4 (1)
Social   level 3 (1)
Security   level 2 (1)
Survival   level 1 (1)
Remember that level 1 needs to be achieved before level 2, etc.

4 They could involve the workers in decision making (1) or training to a higher-level job. (1) You could also include perks that would show that the worker had status like a company car.

5 Hygiene factors were identified by Herzberg as things that made workers demotivated. (1) They included poor pay and conditions. (1) Always try and name the theorist, some exam boards would give an extra mark for this.

6 Give people more responsibility. (1) You could also have said give people promotion or show that they are appreciated.

7 Y (1)

8 **B** He believed a follower of theory X would think that workers enjoyed doing as little as possible. (1) McGregor did not believe in theory X or Y workers. Managers had a theory X or theory Y point of view.

9 You could include:
Excellent rewards offered to the right candidate. (1)
Do you enjoy making decisions? (1)

TOTAL

Check yourself answers

7 REWARDING EMPLOYEES (PAGE 27)

1 Pay. (1)
Fringe benefits. (1)
Incentives. (1)
You may see fringe benefits called perks or incentives called bonuses.

2 Time rate ——————→ Paid by the amount produced (1)

Bonus payments ——————→ Paid by the hour (1)

Piece rate ——————→ Fixed amount because of high profits (1)

3 Overtime pay (1)

4 £7.50 (1) That is, $1\frac{1}{2}$ times £5.00.

5 Time rate. (1)
Piece rate. (1)
Time rate does not encourage speed or quality. Piece rate encourages workers to make as many items as possible.

6 Time rate. (1)
An incentive such as profit-related pay. (1)
An annual salary is the most likely method of payment with a bonus dependent on how profitable the business has been that year.

7 The most likely perks are a subsidised canteen (1) and reduced price goods. (1) Other perks are possible such as health insurance but this is less common.

8 Commission is an incentive (1) to sell as many goods as possible for which a % of the value will be paid. (1)

9 Performance-related pay is an additional sum of money paid for achieving (1) or exceeding a target. (1)

10 Profit-related pay. (1)
A company car. (1) At this level of job a company car is usually given. Do not give a company car as a perk for production workers. There are other acceptable benefits such as health insurance, etc.

TOTAL

Check yourself answers

8 SOURCES OF FNANCE (PAGE 32)

1 When a business is being created. (1)
To replace old equipment. (1)
When a business needs to cover poor cash flow. (1)
For expansion of product range. (1)
For expansion in number of premises. (1)
2 External. (1) This is money from outside the business.

3 **B** Profit from previous years kept in the business (1)

4 By taking on additional partners. (1)
Using the owner's own savings. (1)
They could also use retained profit if there was any.
5 There is no interest to pay. (1) Interest is a major cost for many businesses so this is a very valuable source.
6 **A** Trade credit. (1)
C Overdraft. (1)
7 Any three of the following: Charities, (1) Government, (1) Local council (1) or the EC (1). Grants are a very useful source of finance as no interest is involved.
8 Having to share decisions. (1)
Share profit. (1)
9 By getting a mortgage on the premises. (1)
Using retained profit if there is enough. (1)
Selling existing premises and leasing them back. (1)
There are other sources of finances that such a business could use including: debentures, long-term bank loans, hire purchase or leasing of equipment. In an exam with a case study try and use the information that is given to you. For example, if it says that the business is profitable then it is sensible to suggest retained profit.

TOTAL

Check yourself answers

9 BUSINESS PLANS (PAGE 35)

1 A business plan is a document produced by the owners setting out a business proposal (1) giving information about the business and targets to aim for. (1)

2 To check against targets. (1)
To see where things could have been improved. (1)

3 **C** Value of goods sold last month. (1)
E Copies of recent advertisements. (1)
These would only exist once the business was up and running.

4 What the assets are (1) and their value. (1) This information is needed to see if there is any *collateral* in the business, that is, things that could be sold and the money used to cover the borrowing.

5 Cash flow forecast. (1)
Break-even forecast. (1)
Remember both of these are forecasts made before the business is begun.

6 To see if the predictions of sales are accurate. (1)
That there is a proven demand for the goods. (1)

7 Financial information must be accurate (1) and realistic. (1)
It must not be too optimistic since a high proportion of businesses fail in their first year.

8 The owners should look at the products (1) and the marketing mix of the competition. (1) The business will need to be different from its competitors.

9 To see if the business is worth investing in (1) and has been well planned. (1) To check against targets (1) and to look at areas that could be improved. (1)

TOTAL

1 Running cost → Cost that varies with the amount produced (1)

Total costs → Costs that occur when the business is trading (1)

Variable cost → Sum of fixed and variable costs (1)

Setting-up cost → Costs that remain the same however many items are produced (1)

Fixed cost → Costs involved in setting up a business (1)

2 Electricity (1) and wages (1) can be fixed or variable. This depends whether they are directly involved in production of the goods. If they are then they will be variable costs.

3 It is helpful because it can be a target as it is the point from which profit will be made, (1) and the business can see if this target is likely to be attainable. (1) It is also helpful because the business can see the effect of possible changing costs and revenues. (1)

4

Break-even table for pine chairs				
Sales	FC	VC	TC	TR
0	2500	0	2500	0
25	**2500**	250	**2750**	1500
50	2500	500	3000	**3000**
75	2500	**750**	3250	4500

(5)

5 Variable cost = £6 + £4 = £10 (1)

$$\text{Break even} = \frac{\text{Fixed costs}}{\text{Price per unit} - \text{Variable cost}} \quad (1)$$

$$= \frac{900}{25 - 10} \; (1) \; = \frac{900}{15} \; (1) = 60 \text{ tables} \quad (1)$$

You must show your working or you may not get full marks.

TOTAL

1 Cash inflow → Flow of money out of the business (1)

Cash outflow → Inflows are greater than outflows (1)

Cash surplus → Inflows are smaller than outflows (1)

Cash deficit → Flow of money into the business (1)

It is important that you learn and then use the right terms in your Business Studies examination.

2 A cash flow forecast is a prediction (1) of the money coming into (1) and going out of the business. (1) Note that it is a prediction not an actual situation.

3 Predicting the cash flow helps a business as it can help to spot potential problems. (1) It can then arrange a loan to cover any deficits. (1) A bank manager would expect to see a cash flow forecast with the business plan. (1)

4

	Jan	Feb	Mar	Apr
Bank balance b/f	2000	**6000**	4000	−1000
Cash receipts	12 000	10 000	8000	8000
Total cash in	**14 000**	16 000	12 000	**7000**
Payments/cash out	8000	12 000	**13 000**	8000
Bank balance c/f	**6000**	**4000**	−1000	**−1000**

(7)

5 This cash flow forecast shows that the business is predicting that it will have a surplus in January and February. (1) However, there is a big drop in March when there is a big difference between cash receipts and cash out. (1) This leads to a deficit in March and April. (1)

TOTAL

12 BUSINESS FINANCE (PAGE 51)

1 The stakeholders. (1) These include shareholders, employees and the bank.

2 The value of the stock that has been sold. (1)

3 Gross profit = Sales revenue – Cost of sales
= £12 000 (1) – £6000 (1)
= £6000 (1)
Net profit = Gross profit – Expenses
= £6000 – £3000 (1)
= £3000 (1)
Or the calculation can be done as:
Net profit = Sales revenue – Cost of sales – Expenses

4 Gross profit : Sales revenue = 12 000 (1) : 8000 (1)
= 12 : 8 (1)
= 3 : 2 (1)
Remember to show all the stages in case you make an error in your calculations.

5 $\text{ROCE} = \dfrac{\text{Net profit (1)} \times 100\% \ (1)}{\text{Total capital employed (1)}}$

6 Capital. (1)
Assets. (1)
Liabilities. (1)

7 They show the ability of a business to pay its debts. (1)

8 1.5 : 1 (1) so that the business has sufficient assets to pay its debts in the short term and has not too much money lying idle in its bank account.

9 Stock. (1)

TOTAL

13 MARKET RESEARCH (PAGE 56)

1 To find out about potential customers (1) and reduce the risk. (1) Reducing risk of producing the wrong types of goods or aiming them at the wrong consumers.

2 Desk research   Primary data

Field research   Secondary data (2)

Do not confuse data with research.

3 Desk research. (1) Secondary data. (1)

4 Secondary data. (1)

5 The choice of the correct group of people to ask. (1)
Making sure that the questions are carefully constructed. (1)
The answers will be able to be analysed. (1)
A valid number of people are asked. (1)
If you are asked to discuss the usefulness of some research done by a business you will need to consider the above points in detail.

6 Primary (1)

7 Open (1) Closed questions provide a set of possible answers.

8 Qualitative information is given in depth (1) and is not easily graphed (1) but quantitative information is easily added up (1) and can be used to produce graphs. (1)

9 Random. (1)
Quota. (1)
Targeted. (1)

TOTAL

1 A combination of the marketing mix (1) that is product, price, promotion and place (1) used to meet the business's objectives. (1)

2 Diversification (1)

3 By using trade marks. (1) This is an example of an external legal influence on business behaviour.

4 Price discrimination — Charging below the cost price to attract people into the store

Creaming — Charging different amounts for the same product to different groups of consumers

Penetration pricing — Charging a high price for a new product

Loss leaders — Charging a very low price to get a share of the market

(4)

5 The Advertising Standards Authority. (1)

6 False. (1) One advertisement is produced on behalf of the whole industry.

7 It can be targeted at a particular group of customers (1) and is likely to be re-read as it is published monthly. (1) Remember that the advertisement must be appropriate to the product and within the amount that the business can afford to spend.

8 The main disadvantage is the cost. (1)

9 Handling complaints well. (1)
Being polite to the customer at all times. (1)
Allowing exchanges of goods. (1)

10 Breaks bulk (1) by buying from the producer and selling to the retailer (1)

11 From producer to consumer. (1)

TOTAL

1 Launch, (1) growth, (1) maturity, (1) saturation (1) and decline (1) all labelled correctly and shown on a graph with axes (1) and the correct vertical lines marking the stages. (4) The lines should be similar to the diagram in the text but may not have the same gradient as each product will have different sales.

2

Launch	Growth	Maturity	Saturation	Decline
DVD players	Organic food	CDs	Hair dryers	Cassette players

(5)
The product life cycle is constantly changing and by the time you have used this guide you may find that DVD players are not that new. CDs are still increasing in sales but not very rapidly. The sales of hair dryers are pretty constant as most people own one. Because of various food scares and other factors sale of organic food is increasing rapidly. There are many other examples. If you are asked to give an example state the reasons for your choice.

3 By using an extension strategy. (1) Make sure that you can recognise this stage on a graph as you could be given a life cycle graph to comment on.

4 Before the launch of a product. (1)
Before its decline. (1)

5 By making a new colour. (1)
By changing their size. (1)
There are lots of other ways a sweet manufacturer could try to extend their life cycle. The above examples were used by Nestlé with their product, Smarties.

TOTAL

1 Tertiary production — The extraction of raw materials

Primary production — Manufacturing goods

Secondary production — Providing services

(3)

2

Product	Job, batch or flow production
Wedding dress	Job
Size 10 jeans	Batch
Designing a new website	Job
Golf balls	Flow

(4)

3 Waste (1)

4 Just in time (1) JIT can be used on its own as a method of stock control or used as part of production strategy.

5 Cost of setting up the production line. (1)
Hard to make changes to the product. (1)
Lack of motivation of the workers. (1)

6 Kanban (1)

7 By worker. (1)
By machine. (1)
Per hour. (1)

8 By increasing the amount of goods produced. (1)
By improving the quality so fewer errors are made. (1)

9 The amount of time that resources are not used. (1) The resources can be individual ones or refer to the whole factory.

10 Benefits (1) Costs and benefits can affect the business itself, employees or the community in which the business exists. Taking the example of CAM affecting people, it could lead to poor quality goods being produced, less motivated workers who do not take care in their jobs and high unemployment in the local area.

TOTAL

17 QUALITY CONTROL (PAGE 80)

1 Price may be the primary objective (1) because the demand might be very price sensitive (1) or appearance could be important (1) for goods that are following a trend. (1) An example of appearance could be jeans where the style matters more than the weight of the denim used. In an exam additional marks are often given for examples.

2 Legally goods must be as they are described. (1) They must be safe. (1)

3 If the quality is not within the law (1) they would risk being prosecuted (1). If the quality is not what the customer is wanting then sales would fall (1) resulting in less profit (1). If the goods were poorly made (1) then the business would get a poor name or image. (1)

4 Checking at the end (1) or checking at several points during the production process. (1) Both methods result in waste of time or other resources.

5 By attempting to re-make the goods. (1) For example, goods can be re-packaged or perhaps melted down and re-made.

6 Kaizen — The whole organisation is concerned with quality.

Statistical suggest — Discussion groups meet to process control improvements.

Quality circles — Production workers check their machines regularly.

TQM — Attempts are made to continuously improve production methods.

(4)

7 Competitors. (1) Some information can be obtained by closely examining other businesses products.

TOTAL

1 **C** (1) Job production is a method of production that can be used in almost any location as it suits either large-scale or small-scale enterprises.

2 Climate could affect agriculture. (1) Some products need high temperatures, (1) for example sweetcorn (1). You could give lots of other examples such as tourism and the seaside. It is often a good idea to give a couple of examples.

3 Inertia ——————————————— Presence of water for cooling

   Cost ——————————————— Historical reasons

   Labour ——————————————— Rent of the premises

   Infrastructure ——————————————— Skilled workers

   Nature of the product ——————————————— Bulk increasing product

   Geographical ——————————————— Good road network
   (6)

4 Multinational (1)

5 To provide jobs within an area (1) to reduce unemployment (1). Also to improve skills within an area (1) to improve employment prospects for the people living in the area. (1)

6 Businesses need to be able to obtain their raw materials (1) so good road links may be needed to obtain goods. (1) They need to be able to deliver their goods to their customers. (1) They need to have other businesses around such as repairers that can support their own business. (1) It is a good idea to use joining words in sentences, for example 'such as' and 'so', otherwise your answer may be penalised for being a list.

7 **C** (1) The Inland Revenue will provide help but are not a direct source of finance to businesses.

TOTAL

Check yourself answers

19 EXTERNAL ENVIRONMENT (PAGE 91)

1 Social (1)
Legal (1)
Economic (1)
Environmental (1)
Political (1)
Technological (1)
2 Demographic (1) These are examples of social influences.

3 Health and Safety. (1)
Equal opportunities. (1)
4 The employee. (1)
The employer. (1)
5 Consumers are protected by laws such as the Food and Drugs Act (1) which prevents goods that are not fit for public consumption being sold. (1) It also protects consumers from advertising that is not true (1) and describes products incorrectly. (1) There is a lot of other legislation that could be mentioned but a detailed knowledge of individual laws is not required.
6 Monetary (1)

7 Training might be needed which makes the workers feel valued. (1) It could also help them achieve status or self-actualisation.
8 It increases the market that a business can reach. (1)
It is available for 24 hours a day. (1)
9 It could reduce pollution in the area. (1) Remember that most actions have external benefits as well as costs.

TOTAL

Topic	Check yourself	Points out of 20
Ownership and control	1	
Forms of business	2	
Objectives and growth	3	
Recruitment and selection	4	
Training	5	
Motivation	6	
Rewarding employees	7	
Sources of finance	8	
Business plans	9	
Break even	10	
Cash flow forecasts	11	
Business finance	12	
Market research	13	
Marketing mix	14	
Product life cycle	15	
Production methods	16	
Quality control	17	
Location	18	
External environment	19	

Mark your points for each *Check yourself* on the grid and then read across for your grade.

GCSE Grade

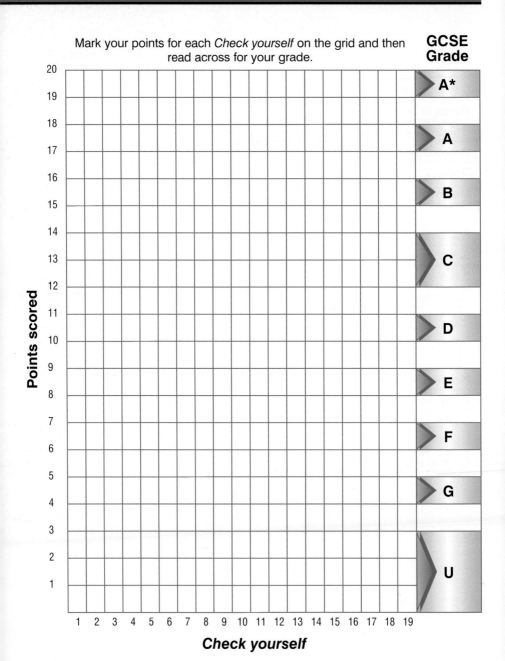